Trauma Has No Color

VOLUME FOUR

A NEW DIMENSION

NARVALEN BAILEY-HAWKINS   DEBORAH JACKSON

CATILIN CROMER   MICHELLE JONES

DAMETRA HAMMOND   NICOLE PIERCE

PATRICIA HOLLINGSWORTH   JASMINE OLIVER

LOGOS

COMMUNITY DEVELOPMENT
CORPORATION

ISBN: 979-8-218-48244-2

Published by Logos CDC

www.logoscdc.org

Harrington, Delaware

Printed in the United States of America

Contents

Forword

In a world that often categorizes and divides, it is easy to forget that some experiences transcend the boundaries we construct. Trauma, in its many forms, does not discriminate; it knows no race, ethnicity, or social status. It is a shared human experience, one that touches lives irrespective of background. This anthology, Trauma Has No Color: A New Dimension, is a testament to the universal yet deeply personal nature of trauma and to the incredible resilience of women who have faced it head-on.

Each narrative within these pages is a powerful reminder of the strength and courage that lies within every woman. These stories are not just about pain and suffering; they are about survival, resilience, and the indomitable spirit that refuses to be crushed. They are stories of reclaiming power, of finding one's voice amidst the silence, and of forging a path towards healing and wholeness.

As you read through this collection, you will encounter a collection of experiences that reflect the diversity of trauma and the myriad ways it manifests in our lives. Yet, you will also see a common thread: the unyielding will to overcome. These women have chosen to share their journeys, not only to unburden their hearts but to inspire others who may be walking similar paths. Their courage in vulnerability is a beacon of hope for all who read their words.

This anthology is more than a collection of stories; it is a movement toward understanding, empathy, and solidarity. It challenges us to look beyond the superficial distinctions that often divide us and to recognize the shared humanity that binds us together. By embracing these stories, we create a bridge that connects our diverse experiences and fosters a community of support and love. It calls us to support one another, to listen with compassion, and to offer kindness and love to those who bear invisible scars.

In celebrating these narratives, we honor the strength of every woman who has dared to face her pain and rise above it. We acknowledge the resilience that defines her and the hope that sustains her. These stories not only highlight individual journeys of recovery but also illuminate the universal potential for renewal and empowerment. Trauma Has No Color: A New Dimension is a powerful affirmation that no matter the color of our skin, the language we speak, or the culture we come from, we all have the capacity to heal, to thrive, and to transform our pain into power.

May these stories inspire you, move you, and remind you that in the shared experience of trauma, we find not only pain but also profound connection and strength. To every woman who has contributed her story to this anthology, thank you for your bravery and your voice. Your courage helps to break the silence and paves the way for others to find their own paths to healing. You are a testament to the fact that while trauma may touch us all, it is our response to it that defines us.

With deep respect and admiration,

~ *Dr. Teneshia T. Winder PhD, LMFT*

CHAPTER ONE

The Southern Westcoast Phoenix

Narvalen Bailey-Hawkins

As I reflect on my past, I can remember the day as if it were yesterday. The sky was overcast, shrouded in a thick fog that made the air feel chilly. Birds chirped and flew through the mist, their songs the only sounds breaking the eerie stillness. From the window, I watched my mom and dad getting my sister and me dressed for the day. It was park day, our favorite. My sister and I loved feeding the ducks and playing on the swings. Those moments with my family were filled with so much love and joy. I felt like the happiness we had would last forever.

Growing up with both parents at home, I thought I had the perfect life. My parents never argued in front of us; there was always love, or so it seemed. My childhood felt safe and happy, filled with moments of laughter and family time. I believed this happiness would last forever. But then, things started to change, and my perfect world began to fall apart. My dad, who used to be home all the time, started coming home less often. At first, it was just a few late nights here and there. I would ask my mom where he was, and she would give vague answers, trying to reassure me with a smile that didn't quite reach her eyes. But as the days without him grew longer, I couldn't shake the feeling that something was wrong. I tried to ignore the growing void, convincing myself that everything was fine. But kids can tell when something is wrong, and I could feel the tension building. My mom tried to act like everything was normal, but I could see the worry in her eyes and the way she seemed to be carrying a heavy burden.

One day, my mom sat us down and said, "We're moving to a different place, and your dad isn't coming with us." My whole world shattered right then and there. I was just a kid, and I couldn't understand what was happening. The sadness that followed was overwhelming. I adored my dad and believed my parents were happy. Little did I know our lives were about to change in ways I could never have imagined. Whatever lay ahead, I had a sinking feeling it wouldn't end well.

As soon as my mom said those words, I felt like everything was falling apart. I loved my dad so much and couldn't imagine life without him around. I always thought my parents were happy and that we were a perfect family. Hearing that we were moving without him made me feel like the ground had been ripped out from under me. It was like everything I knew and loved was suddenly falling apart.

In the days that followed, the sadness turned into a constant, heavy weight on my chest. I kept hoping it was all a bad dream, that I would wake up and everything would be back to normal. But as we packed up our things and the moving day got closer; reality sank in deeper. I could see the pain in my mom's eyes, too, but I didn't know how to talk about it. I felt alone in my sadness, unable to understand why this was happening.

The move itself was a blur of boxes and goodbyes. I remember clinging to the hope that maybe things would get better, that my dad would come back, and everything would be okay again. But deep down, I had a sinking feeling that our lives were about to change in ways I couldn't imagine, and not for the better. It felt like I was standing on the edge of a cliff, staring into an uncertain and scary future.

Born on April 6, 1980, my life started off in the sunny landscapes of Los Angeles, California, with a seasoning of Greenville, South Carolina charm. My family was the picture of happiness to my young eyes. With a younger sister to tag along, I was the trailblazer of our little duo. Mom was the superstar of our household, showering us with love and care. Dad was more like a background presence, but his support was always felt. My earliest and happiest memories include simple pleasures like feeding ducks at the park across from our house and enjoying the beach that was a mere five-minute trek from our Playa Del Rey home. Those moments were pure bliss—free, fun, and utterly safe.

But as life would have it, things started to change as I grew older. The bond with my sister, however, only grew stronger. We were inseparable, the best of friends, with me always watching over her. Our adventures extended to South Carolina, where we got to meet more of our extended family, adding a couple of cool cousins into our mix and deepening our sense of belonging. Our independence kicked a notch higher when we began flying by ourselves to visit Dad's side of the family. It was during these visits that we stumbled upon family secrets and unspoken stories, like the uncle who mysteriously never returned from California, later revealed to be due to his incarceration—a fact kept hush-hush under the family's code of silence.

Childhood wasn't just about navigating family relationships; it was also about finding my own voice among the complexities of growing up. When family tensions surfaced, I felt sidelined, unable to express my desires or concerns. When I visited relatives in South Carolina, I saw a lot of arguing and tension, which was totally different from the calm atmosphere we usually had at home. This made me feel alone and unsupported, and I started wondering where I fit into the family and why I felt like I wasn't good enough.

Even with all these problems, the core values my parents taught me—respect, kindness, and dignity—kept guiding me. My mom was especially good at this. She always reminded us of our worth and beauty and how important faith is. Her words were like a safe place for me, giving me comfort and strength when things got tough.

My school life was just as complicated as my home life. I dealt with bullying by girls and petty jealousy. The more they targeted me, the more isolated I felt. Despite the bullying, I tried to put on a brave face. I didn't want to give them the satisfaction of knowing how much their words hurt. The pain was real, and it left scars that took time to heal. I vividly recall one incident when this girl, whom I thought was my friend, called my house and left a nasty message on the answering machine. I could not believe the nasty things she said. In those days, house phones were the thing, not cell phones. Slowly but surely, I learned to set boundaries and distanced myself from toxic individuals. Although school was tough, I also found genuine connections and friendships. I learned the value of authenticity and the power of resilience. These interactions taught me the importance of standing up for myself and seeking out true, genuine connections despite the "Petty Betties"!

I was always getting into trouble, but no one really took the time to explain what I was doing wrong. Instead of talking things through, I'd get punished or yelled at. During this time, my sister and I were living in South Carolina with my aunt on my dad's side. The relationships I had there were complex—some were good for me, and some were harmful. I remember being bullied for no reason, which just made me crave acceptance and friendship even more. Despite trying to be kind and make friends, I often got hostility in return, and I ended up fighting a lot just to defend myself. This push and pull of wanting to fit in but being pushed away made me put up walls and act tough to protect myself from anyone who tried to mess with me.

The adults in my life didn't seem to notice or didn't know how to help. When I got into fights, they saw me as the troublemaker. No one sat me down to ask why I was fighting or to understand my side of the story. I was punished, grounded, or yelled at, which only added to my frustration and feelings of isolation. This cycle of trying to fit in, getting bullied, and then getting in trouble for fighting made me feel hopeless. I started to believe that the only way to survive was to act tough and keep people at a distance. I thought if I showed any vulnerability, it would just be used against me. So, I built walls around myself, pretending not to care about anyone or anything.

I've had my share of trauma throughout my life, but one experience stands out the most for me. Around the age of 6 or 7 years old, a time when you'd expect nothing more than scraped knees and ice cream stains on your shirt. My parents were going through a rough patch, the kind you don't really get when you're that young, just that the air at home felt heavier, and suddenly, my sister and I were packing bags for grandma's. The thrill, joy, and sheer happiness that filled me at the thought of spending time with our grandmother and being with family was beyond words. I never imagined, not in a million years, that I would find myself feeling numb and disconnected from who I was. The idea was simple: visit, have fun, get spoiled, and come back home to California with a bunch of happy stories to tell my parents.

Grandma's house was always busy because it was known as the candy house in the neighborhood. My grandmother sold everything from candy and chips to ice pops, beer, and chili cheese Fritos, among other things. My sister and I would spend hours playing outside in the front yard—tag, digging in the dirt, and simply enjoying each other's company. She would often suggest games like a red light, green light, or Simon Says, and we always found a way to make the best of our time together. Occasionally, our cousin would join us for play or sleepovers, although my sister and I were never allowed to spend the night elsewhere or venture too far from Grandma's apartment. I always sensed that my sister and I were different, coming from a larger place, which somehow made us stand out and be treated differently. Despite this, we remained true to ourselves, always treating others with love and kindness.

However, what was meant to be an amazing stay at Grandma's took a sharp turn, becoming cold, dark, and unfamiliar. As I recall those moments that changed my life forever, I remember my grandmother asleep on the couch. My uncle told me to go into the bedroom, and I didn't think anything was wrong because it wasn't unusual for me to be sent to my room. The bedroom was down the hall on the left. The room was dark but slightly lit by the television that my sister was watching. There were bunk beds to the left of the door and an entertainment center with a television in front of a chair. My sister was sitting in the chair, absorbed in the show, and never turning around to see who entered the room. The door shut behind me, and he told me to lie on the bed. It wasn't normal. It wasn't normal; I thought he wanted to go into the room to watch television. Something didn't feel right; something was off, and before I even had time to process it, he had already begun to rub my leg and touch my breast.

I didn't know what was happening to me. His hands felt so horrible on my body. They were moving so fast that I could not stop them. So many things were going through my mind. I didn't feel like I could make him stop. He asked me if I wanted to feel something, and before I could respond, he took my hand and made me touch and rub him. He asked if I had ever been licked on, and I said no. I was tense and confused. I could feel him trying to penetrate me and could not get it all the way in. He pushed me down and tried to make me give him oral sex. I had no idea what was happening to me. I felt a mix of fear, confusion, and helplessness. I was terrified and couldn't make sense of what was happening.

The experience of sexual abuse shattered my sense of safety and trust completely. I felt like I couldn't trust anyone, not even myself. I doubted my judgment and instincts because I couldn't understand how I ended up in such a situation. I became hyper-vigilant, always on edge, and constantly second-guessing people's intentions. It took me a long time to feel safe again, and even now, I struggle with trusting others fully.

I found myself struggling with a secret, fearful of putting my sister in harm's way. Our relationship transitioned into one of protection and vigilance. I couldn't bear the thought of leaving her alone, scared of the potential harm that could happen to her. This worry made it nearly impossible to relax. My sister was, and still is my best friend, and I was determined to do whatever it took to shield her from being molested. While we were at grandma's house, my uncle had begun molesting me. I couldn't wait to get out of there and go back home.

This silence made me struggle on my own, keeping up a front of being okay when inside, I was anything but. You know that saying, "What goes on in this house stays in this house?" Yes, that was a true statement. I suffered in silence, having to save face to portray this person I was. Initially, I was a happy kid—free and full of love. I was always smiling and so excited about life. I quickly learned how to wear a mask. I learned how to hide my real feelings of being broken, lost, and angry. By day, I acted normal, but at night, I'd be overwhelmed with tears. This double life made me feel like a fraud like I was pretending to be someone I wasn't. The abuse severely damaged my sense of self-worth. I felt worthless and believed I didn't deserve good things in life. It took a lot of work in therapy to rebuild my self-esteem. Regarding personal boundaries, the abuse made me either overly rigid or too lenient with them. I struggled to find a balance. I often felt like I had to please others to be accepted, which meant I didn't always respect my own boundaries. Learning to assert my boundaries has been a crucial part of my recovery and has helped me regain a sense of control and respect for myself.

Despite this, I couldn't let my guard down; I had to be the person everyone thought I was, even though I felt completely alone and misunderstood. Being from California, while the rest of my family was in South Carolina, only made these feelings of being an outsider worse. When I interacted with others, it felt like they were just going through the motions, not really connecting with me. Out of fear that speaking up might hurt my sister, I put on an act, taking on the "troublemaker" role because it was easier to meet those expectations than to show my real struggles. This persona was so unlike me—angry, withdrawn, and reckless. It was a lonely fight, surrounded by people but feeling deeply alone.

The person I saw in the mirror felt like a stranger, carrying burdens that were too much for someone my age. I was super loud, just trying to get any kind of attention to cover up the quiet around what I had lost. But underneath all that noise, it was just me—lost in my thoughts, hoping for something or someone to pull me out of that deep, lonely place. This period was like a storm that changed everything about my early years and left me with scars that remind me of past hurts and what could have been.

My sister and I thought we were heading back home after a summer visit. But when it was time to leave, we didn't go to the airport. Instead, I remember the police leading us out of my grandmother's house with my aunt and three police cars there. We were totally lost, not understanding what was going on; we just thought we were going home. That's when my aunt showed some papers to the police, which turned out to be guardianship documents from my mother. She was going to take care of us for a while. I felt an enormous sense of relief and gratitude at that moment; I had never been so thankful to be "rescued." If my sister and I had to stay any longer, I was sure my uncle would've continued to molest me.

I started to realize at age twelve that I was attracted to the same sex. This realization added layers of confusion to my already complex life. At such a young age, I had no understanding of what these feelings meant, and there was no one I could turn to for guidance. The fear of being different from my peers made me feel isolated and scared. I didn't know how to process these emotions, and I felt like I had to hide a part of myself, which only deepened my sense of confusion and loneliness.

As I entered my teenage years, this confusion manifested in increasingly rebellious behavior. My behavior became more and more uncontrollable. I was acting out in ways that were destructive and reckless, desperately trying to escape the emotional turmoil I was experiencing. I was lost, trying to find comfort in anything that would numb the pain and confusion I felt inside, which is why I turned to drugs and sex. My mother, at her wit's end, decided to send me to a tough love group home, hoping that the strict environment would correct my behavior. The group home wasn't exactly warm and cozy. The strict rules and rigid routines were meant to teach discipline and responsibility, but to me, they often felt more like punishment. Adjusting to this new environment was really tough. I was separated from my family and placed in a setting where every aspect of my behavior was constantly monitored.

Living in the group home was one of the hardest experiences of my life. Every day felt like a battle as I tried to deal with the reality of my situation. The place was set up to make me face my past actions and think about my choices, but I was too angry and rebellious to care. Even though it was difficult, the group home did provide a structure I had never experienced before. Despite the rigid structure, I met a friend there, and we decided to run away together. After we ran away, we both got into trouble. With little knowledge about how dangerous things really were, we were in a situation where we almost became victims of human trafficking. Thank God! We were picked up by the police, and I was sent to live with my dad. The reason I ran away was that my mom was supposed to pick me up after my stay at the group home, but I didn't want to go home with her. I was still angry at her for some of the things she did, and I just didn't want to deal with it.

My mom's boyfriend used to beat her up a lot. I got sick of hearing it and seeing her with black eyes. It made me feel so helpless as if there was nothing I could do about it. I remember listening to the sounds of their fights and feeling a mix of fear, anger, and frustration. I didn't understand why she stayed with him or why she let it keep happening. I was angry at my mom for staying with him. It felt like she was choosing him over our safety and happiness. I felt trapped in a situation I couldn't change, watching her get hurt over and over again. Those feelings of anger and helplessness built up inside me, making it impossible for me to go back to her.

After going to my dad's house, I started to feel a little different. What I didn't realize was that I was pregnant. His girlfriend took me to the doctor to confirm it, and there it was—positive. I didn't know what to think; I was unsure how to handle this. Instead of finding the support and guidance I desperately needed, I was met with rejection. Instead of helping me navigate through this unexpected turn, my dad's girlfriend told my dad I couldn't stay. Just like that, I was sent back to my mother. I wasn't sure how she was going to respond because the first time I got pregnant, she made me have an abortion. I was sixteen and four months pregnant. This time was different; I actually had my son, Brandon, and he was amazing. Just like that, I became a mom.

In my early twenties, life was a chaotic blur. The days and nights are grouped into one continuous stream of partying and dealing with my mom's terrible boyfriend and moving us all around. There was no stability at all. The uncertainty and instability at home added layers of stress and confusion to my already chaotic life. Amidst this chaos, having my son at 16 was a life-changing moment. Part of me felt overwhelmed, another part felt joy, and the other part of me was terrified of being a young mother. I felt a huge sense of responsibility but was also scared of the future and how I would provide for him.

From ages 23 to 26, my life was an emotional rollercoaster. I had my daughter and started dating a woman for the first time, which was a new and confusing experience. I was actually messing around with girls at the age of seventeen, and I started dating this one girl who I thought was the one. That wasn't the case. The woman I had my first relationship with was great in the beginning until it wasn't. Our relationship was full of constant fighting and moving from place to place. This instability made everything feel out of control, and it started to affect me and my children deeply. Each day felt uncertain, and the stress of it all was overwhelming.

I was exhausted, both physically and emotionally, from trying to keep everything together while dealing with the ups and downs of my relationship. I wanted to give my children a stable and happy home, but I felt like I was failing. The chaotic environment was not what they deserved, and I knew I had to do something to protect them. After much thought, I sent them to live with my aunt. The decision to leave my kids with a trusted family member was the hardest thing I've ever done. My aunt was the one who helped my mom rescue us from her mother. I just knew my kids were safe, loved, and treated kindly, but what could I expect from the same women who used to cuss me and my cousins out if we got in trouble or made a mistake? I learned some years down the line how my children were really treated, but with that said, it broke my heart to think about being away from them. I felt like I was letting them down and abandoning my responsibilities as their mother.

I spent many sleepless nights crying and questioning if I was making the right choice. The guilt and sadness were almost unbearable, but I believed it was the only way to keep them safe. During this time, I struggled with feelings of failure and sadness. I wondered if I was a good enough mother and if I had made the right choices. But deep down, I knew that sometimes the hardest decisions are the ones we make out of love. By keeping my children away from the chaos, I was trying to give them the peace and security I couldn't provide at that moment.

By the time I hit 32, I had already endured two painful breakups that left me feeling emotionally drained and uncertain about the future. These breakups took a toll on my self-esteem and left me questioning my worth and ability to maintain a healthy relationship. Just as I was trying to navigate through this emotional wreckage, the unthinkable happened—my mom passed away on Mother's Day in 2011. The grief was unbearable. Losing her shattered me in ways I couldn't have imagined. She was my rock, my confidant, and her sudden absence left a void that felt impossible to fill.

The pain of losing my mom was so intense that it felt like a physical ache. I was overwhelmed with a sense of loneliness and despair. I struggled to mourn properly; I couldn't find the time or the space to process my grief amidst the chaos of daily life. I felt as if I was drowning in sorrow, with no one to pull me out. To cope, I buried myself in work, hoping that staying busy would distract me from the pain. I threw myself into my job, working long hours and taking on extra responsibilities. But no matter how hard I worked, the grief was always there, lurking in the background, waiting to engulf me.

When work wasn't enough to numb the pain, I turned to drinking and smoking. Alcohol became a way to escape, even if just for a little while. I started smoking more, trying to calm the anxiety that seemed to follow me everywhere. I also found myself drawn into toxic relationships, seeking comfort and distraction in all the wrong places. These relationships were filled with drama and conflict, adding more stress to an already overwhelming situation.

All the while, I was barely holding it together for my kids, who were dealing with their own health issues. They needed me to be strong and present, but I felt like I was failing them. The weight of trying to manage my grief, my unhealthy coping mechanisms, and my responsibilities as a mother was crushing. I often felt like I was on the brink of falling apart, struggling to keep everything together with sheer willpower. Despite the chaos, there was a small part of me that knew I had to find a way out of this dark place. I couldn't continue down this path of self-destruction. My kids needed me, and I owed it to them and to myself to find a way to heal and move forward.

Between the ages of 35 and 43, I decided it was time to turn my life around. I reconnected with my best friend, who brought a sense of stability and hope back into my life. Eventually, we got married, and together, we didn't want to have a long-distance relationship or marriage, so we decided it would be great to move to Delaware for a fresh start. My wife was still on active duty at the time. I believed a new environment could be the key to a better future for my family.

But starting over wasn't as easy as I had hoped. My oldest son was having a hard time; he struggled with self-harm and faced challenges in college. My youngest was constantly getting into trouble, testing boundaries, and pushing limits. My daughter was caught in the middle, trying to figure out her place in our complicated family dynamic. It was a tough time for all of us, and I often felt overwhelmed by their struggles and my own unresolved issues.

Despite my best efforts to create a stable home, I was still battling my own demons. The pain from my past continued to haunt me, making it difficult to fully support my kids the way they needed. It also affected my marriage. I often felt offended and took most things my spouse said or did as a personal attack against me. I struggled to understand their needs, partially because I couldn't even understand my own. My inability to provide emotional support strained our relationship and made it hard for us to truly connect with each other.

I realized that I couldn't keep going like this—I had to take control of my life and start healing from the inside out. I came to understand that my past didn't have to define me. Seeking help and working on myself became a priority. It was a long but transforming journey, filled with ups and downs, but it was necessary. I learned that change is possible, no matter how late it might seem. Now, I'm focused on creating a better future for myself and my family. I'm determined to break free from the patterns of the past and build a more hopeful and stable life. It hasn't been easy, but I've come to believe that it's never too late to change the narrative and strive for something better. I've learned that I am the author of my story, and no one gets the right to write the ending but me!

LETTER TO SELF

Dear Narvalen,

I know you had a trying time in your life experiences and childhood growing up. I know you felt scared, abandoned, unloved and alone. You were never responsible for all the things that happened to you. The pain you bore was unfair and underserved. I am here to let you know that your past does not define you as a person. It was not your fault your parents separated or that you moved around from place to place. It was not your fault your uncle molested you or your family members treated you like a black sheep. You are so much stronger than the life experiences you have had that happened to you. You are a survivor and still here to tell your story. Your resilience shines so brightly. You have the power to break barriers and chains that hold onto you. You are not your trauma. Give yourself grace and love, and remember that you made the conscious decision to heal. You are a living testament to being strong and having the courage to face this head-on. Speak life into yourself, embrace the beautiful person you become, and give yourself permission to keep growing beyond your trauma.

Celebrate your progress, honor your efforts, and cherish the love and support that comes your way. You are resilient and a woman who has persevered through life struggles. You are the strongest person I know. You have come through the storms with your head held high and with more confidence that exudes through you. You have taken your power and your voice back. Give yourself grace and create space for all things God is giving to you. Healing is a process, not a race. Never give up on yourself. Keep reaching new heights in your life. Live, love, laugh. You are in control of your destiny and, most importantly, your future. You are a Queen that never gives up. I am so proud of you.

Narvalen. Remember, keep allowing yourself to grow beyond measures. Never stop and give space to continue to heal. I love you. You are doing it, and you are manifesting all you deserve. Keep on keeping on, cause skies are the limit.

Love your older self,

~ Narvalen

CHAPTER TWO

Whispering Shadows:

A Journey Within

Catilin Cromer

Chaos, instability, abuse, death, trauma, and brokenness—
these were the constants of my life. The pieces of our fractured
family were scattered everywhere, sharp and painful. Navigating
through this minefield of emotions, each step was panic-stricken,
fraught with the danger of uncovering even more pain. The loss
of a loved one only deepened the wounds, leaving us more
fragmented than ever.

Yet, amidst the chaos and instability, amidst the abuse and
death, amidst the trauma and brokenness, I began to see
something else. The shattered pieces of our lives, like the
fragments of a broken mirror, held the potential for something
new. Each jagged edge was a part of our story, a piece of the past

that, when put together with care, could form an intricate and beautiful mosaic. My journey was about more than just surviving the pain—it was about finding a way to transform those shattered pieces into a work of art.

Every shard of our shattered lives contributed to a mosaic that was priceless. I invite you to journey with me through the pages of this art museum that showcases the work of art that I call my life. Here, in this narrative, you will see the beauty that emerged from the brokenness, the strength forged in the fires of adversity, and the hope that I held on to in the midst of the ruins. Welcome to my story, my masterpiece, my life.

I was born in Dover, Delaware, the only place I've ever known. Like many others, I've always dreamed of leaving and seeing the world beyond my doorstep. Wanting to leave my hometown was my way of escaping everything and everyone. The idea was simple: the further away, the better. I wasn't concerned about who or what I was leaving behind. I've always dreamed of traveling to a place where I can truly breathe and be myself. Greece has always been at the top of my list. Just looking at pictures of its stunning landscapes fills me with joy. It's a place where I feel I could lose myself and find myself all at once.

My family's story is one of complexity and brokenness. My biological mother, in her search for stability, shifted from my father to another man, leaving us in a state of constant upheaval.

I am the second oldest of five siblings, stuck right in the middle of our chaotic family dynamic. The sense of brokenness in my family was pervasive. It seemed like problems were always cropping up, and nothing was ever truly resolved—just discarded like trash. Rarely did happy moments last long. However, there was an exception: my siblings. Despite our occasional fights, we always managed to resolve our conflicts. They were my rock and my center. My older sister and I weren't always close, but something clicked one day, and from then on, we were inseparable. Together, we took on the role of parents for our younger siblings. While I was the fun-loving one, she enforced the rules. It was us against the world, united and strong.

Growing up, my mother was a constant presence, while my father was a figure of absence and disappointment. When he was around, he was either drinking or trying to play the role of a father, a role so foreign to me. My father alternated between being a hero and a villain in the narrative of my life. Now, with 19 months of sobriety to his name, we're slowly mending our relationship. My mother, on the other hand, battled her own demons, leaving little room for my problems. Our relationship has always been a rollercoaster, marked by small moments of peace that were quickly overshadowed by Chaos.

One of my earliest memories is the struggles and eventual triumph of learning to ride a bike, paint a picture of my childhood's challenges and small victories. Learning how to ride a bike was incredibly freeing, but mastering it on my own was even more empowering. It taught me that I could accomplish anything once I managed to conquer my fears. Having my uncle there during this significant moment gave me a cherished memory, especially since we lost him so young. His support during this time meant more to me than anything I could have expected from my birth mother. Conversely, it also taught me the harsh lesson of not giving up or walking away when faced with challenges or pain.

Around the age of nine or ten, I remember a particularly foggy memory about my uncle. It was a regular day, and because our house didn't have central air conditioning, we all slept downstairs in the living room, where a box air conditioner unit was set up. I loved it because it felt like a huge slumber party. The house was so hot it felt like a sauna. The sound of that air conditioner was loud, and I recall the carpet being wet from the condensation.

That next morning, when we woke up, everything seemed different. People were upset, some were crying, and things were not normal. I kept asking what had happened, but no one could give me a straight answer. Then, suddenly, this person—whom I typically refer to as "the stray" that my mom picked up from the street—blurted out, "Your uncle committed suicide." My mom had a habit of bringing home people who needed a place to stay or wanted to help out, but she never considered how these strangers might make our home unsafe. The stray was an insignificant person in our family, yet his words hit me like a punch to the gut. Hearing that my uncle had committed suicide was confusing to me. I was nine years old, and I didn't even understand what suicide meant. As I sought out understanding, the "stray" explained that my uncle had taken his own life. Those words stripped me of the feeling that I had in my body, and I instantly became numb. I was in shock and disbelief, feeling all my emotions at once.

I can't remember much of what happened next as the family began to prepare for the funeral. It wasn't much of a funeral; we went to the funeral home and saw my uncle's body lying on a table. He smelled a little strange, but he looked nice. I didn't want to go up there, but I was forced to. I remember thinking I just wanted to go home. After we saw him on that table, he was cremated. Just like that, he was erased, gone forever.

Everyone seemed so sad and confused, but I didn't understand why. My uncle had an addiction problem and was often seen as the black sheep of the family. I felt like no one really cared about him when he was alive; they just felt guilty now that they couldn't help him anymore. I have fond memories of my uncle being really fun. He would always take me places, and he lived in a van on our property. It didn't seem weird at the time; he was always there for me. I feel sad because I think he suffered alone. I don't know everything that transpired within the family that led them to treat him the way they did, but I still don't think he should have suffered alone.

Shortly after he died, it was strange to see people start fighting over his things. It was as if they went from feeling sad that he wasn't there to wondering what they could get from his belongings. I really wanted him to come back. My uncle had been in a lot of foster homes because my grandparents also had addiction problems, so he was dealt a difficult path from the start. He never had a sense of stability. I can't imagine how he must have felt being tossed from one home to another; he had to be lonely.

No one really talks about him anymore, and that bothers me. It's almost like people have forgotten him. I know that he loved me, and I wish I had more time to get to know him. One thing I can take away from this experience is the importance of not repeating the same mistakes. Although my uncle struggled, I want to make different choices and ensure that I lead a life with more stability and support.

Shortly after my uncle's death, the insignificant "stray" became very significant." One evening, my sister, her friend, and I were hanging out at the house. I faintly remember this stray that my mom brought home and gave us all a pill to take. He told us that the pill would make us feel relaxed. I remember feeling a little paralyzed and dizzy. The next thing I remember was waking up in my room the next morning. I don't know how I got in my bed. Apparently, my sister and her friend had been molested by this person. They remembered everything. I'm not really sure what was going through my sister's mind when this happened, as I was very confused by what happened shortly after.

My sister was texting someone on the phone and would not let me see the messages. Acting as any younger sister might, I complained to our mom about being treated unfairly. My mother grabbed her phone and saw that she was actually texting the "stray" that she bought home. All of a sudden, everything that had happened to us the night we were drugged came out. The police were called, and that "stray" was arrested and jailed. He kept apologizing as he was being handcuffed and placed in the police car.

Looking back, I'm grateful I spoke up because my actions led to the arrest of a dangerous man. At just nine years old, I didn't fully grasp what was happening. All I knew was that I felt guilty for causing trouble serious enough for the police to get involved. I was terrified during the questioning, unsure if I was saying the wrong things. Afterward, my sister wouldn't speak or eat, and she avoided me for days. I thought she was angry at me.

Years later, as adults, we talked about that day. She expressed gratitude for my actions, telling me that if I hadn't spoken up, the abuse might have continued, causing even more harm. She confessed that she admired my courage and regretted not having the strength to stand up as I did. At the time, she thought what was happening was normal, but she now recognizes it was all a lie.

During my childhood, I struggled deeply, often resorting to isolation and self-harm as coping mechanisms. These methods provided only temporary relief. Self-harm momentarily eased the pain, but it always returned, seemingly stronger each time. Isolation made me feel utterly alone, reinforcing my belief that no one cared or even noticed my distress. I felt invisible as if being out of sight meant I was also out of everyone's mind. A pivotal moment came when my best friend confronted me about my behavior. They told me, "If you keep hiding behind the shadows, you will never be heard. Speak up and be heard. If no one listens, make them." This advice struck a chord with me, and it has guided me ever since. I realized that to change my circumstances, I needed to advocate for myself and express my struggles openly. It's a journey I am still on, learning each day to step out from the shadows and make my voice heard.

In my early teenage years, I often felt invisible at school. Most of my classmates didn't engage with me, and those who did seemed to only want something from me. This led me to prefer being alone, retreating into my own world where I could remain unseen and undisturbed. Initially, I was known as the quiet one, someone who just wanted to get through the day and return home to the safety of invisibility.

However, my attitude began to shift in high school. I used to care deeply about what others thought of me, but this sensitivity only brought me pain and disappointment. Realizing that people would eventually leave my life, I decided to adopt an "I don't care" attitude. This change was a protective measure—a way to preemptively distance myself from others before they could hurt me. This mindset stemmed from deep-seated feelings of abandonment, reinforced by the lack of protection I felt from my own mother against harmful influences in our lives. This transformation deeply affected my interactions with my peers. By not caring, I pushed people away before they could get close enough to leave a mark. It was a defense mechanism, but it also led me to a profound realization of self-reliance and the importance of guarding my emotional well-being.

Relationships with other family members were strained and controlled while living under my mother's roof. I rarely saw extended family, as my mother's preferences dictated our social interactions. My father's family remained mostly a mystery, except for Aunt Kim and Aunt Heather, who provided me with the support and care I desperately needed. I quickly learned that support was something I often had to provide for myself. Not everyone around me realized I needed it, or perhaps they didn't care enough to offer it.

My relationships with family members during my childhood were complex and often strained due to the controlling nature of my biological mother. If she did not want someone around, she would prevent me from seeing them or going anywhere with them, which made interactions with extended family quite rare. Additionally, my mother's family wanted little to do with her, which unfortunately extended to me as well. On my father's side, I didn't know many relatives except for Aunt Kim, one of my father's sisters. Despite having her own family to care for, she did all she could to support me. Our relationship deepened significantly when I moved in with her at the age of 15 after being taken from my mother's custody.

I was also close to my Aunt Heather, who was like the mother I always needed and wanted. Things were easier when she lived with us, but after she and my biological mother had a falling out, she moved far away. Our contact was limited until I got my own phone and could call her whenever I needed. Our relationship improved as my home life deteriorated. Eventually, when she moved back, I moved in with her, my uncle, and their son, which greatly stabilized my life and strengthened our bond.

Aunt Heather was also pivotal during my challenging times. Witnessing much of the abuse I endured, she did her best to protect us, even though she was only nineteen years old herself. We lost touch a few times because my birth mother caused her pain, but Aunt Heather's resilience and care deeply influenced my upbringing. These two women essentially raised me, teaching me everything I needed to know. If I had a choice about who my mother would be, it would have been one of them. Yet, I realize now that their presence was meant to strengthen the bond I share with my siblings—a bond not everyone is fortunate enough to experience.

NOTE TO SELF

Dear Younger Self,

Let go of it all. You can't control what happens to you, only what happens to you. Remember, you are resilient. It's okay to be a kid now; you don't have to worry. I'm here for you. Grow into who you want to be; you are brave and kind. You are enough. You can rest now, knowing everything will be alright. You can overcome anything. Cry, laugh, scream—do anything you feel. No one can tell you what to feel anymore. Feel everything and then let it go. You are loved in so many ways.   With love, Your Older Self ~ Cat

CHAPTER THREE

Echoes of Strength

Dametra Hammond

Life can sometimes feel like being caught in the eye of a hurricane. The calm, deceptive, and temporary can quickly give way to a storm of overwhelming intensity. Abandonment and rejection swirl like violent winds, trauma and abuse strike with the force of crashing waves, and fear, embarrassment, and shame lingers like relentless rain. In the midst of this relentless storm, a heart battered by vicious elements still beats with endurance and faith as it pursues healing.

Echoes of strength that resonate within us all highlight the path from darkness to dawn. These echoes, like whispers of resilience, remind us that survival is not just about enduring the storm but about emerging from it with a renewed and transformed sense of self, power, purpose, and courage. May the echoes of my testimony help give you strength and wisdom as you navigate your storms.

I was born in Seaford, Delaware, at Nanticoke Memorial Hospital. Growing up, I moved a lot, bouncing around places like Milford, Harrington, and Lincoln. That's pretty much where I spent my childhood. I lived in North Carolina for a bit, too, but then I got taken away from my mom's care. My mom has five kids, and I'm smack in the middle. Being the middle child of my mother's five and the youngest of my father's three was good whenever we were together. My mother didn't raise all of her children. I was always the one looking out for us all, even to this day. Everyone assumes I'm the oldest because I have been the glue, trying to keep us all in contact. All I ever wanted was to be with my siblings, but it just became harder and harder.

On my dad's side, though, I'm the youngest of three. I never really got to do much with them. Very rarely did I get a chance to play with them. The only sibling I was very close to was my baby sister, who I just lost on June 15th, 2023. The distance from my siblings was very hard for me. All I ever wanted was the bond of my family.

When it came to my parents, things were okay, I guess. I don't have too many memories with my mom since I was so young. But there are some that stick out the most to me. My earliest memories are from when I was around 3 or 4. I remember walking with my mom down the street. She'd hold my hand, take me to school, we talked, laughed, and smiled. And then there's this memory with my oldest sister – we'd be outside on the porch, playing in a kiddie pool, pretending to catch the Holy Ghost playing church. But sometimes, it felt like we weren't just pretending and started praising God for real.

One summer, my mom sent me and my baby sister back to Delaware to visit our grandma. Thinking we weren't being looked after well enough by our mom, Grandma called my aunt to pick up me and my sister. Sadly, my aunt could only take me, leaving my baby sister behind. I was about to turn 8, and she was almost 5. I felt a mix of happiness to be with my aunt but also hurt because I had to leave my sister. I kept wondering, what's going to happen to her now? My aunt already had a son, three years older than me, and over time, a few of my cousins joined us. She was a spiritual person, and she took care of all of us. She is the one who introduced me to God. She taught me how to pray and lean on God. I watched her in church and at home. She always told me to be independent and that if I wanted something, I should go after it.

The distance from my family taught me that people will come and go. Why would anyone else stick around if my parents didn't want me and left me? I always knew I had to have my own back, and I still do. I am very independent and don't ask anyone for much. I don't have much faith regarding people staying in my life. I knew when people entered my life, it was only going to be for a little while, so I never got too close.

In my youth, I was surrounded by a mix of perspectives and values, thanks to my diverse family. My mom was the free spirit of the bunch, always encouraging me to be myself and live my truth, no matter what. It was a different story on my dad's side, though—that's where I got to know God. They introduced me to the church, teaching me that prayer is more than words; it's a weapon! While I saw my aunt, grandmother, and great-grandmother mostly practicing what they preached, there were times when their actions didn't quite match up with their words. It wasn't across the board, but it seemed like they weren't fully living out the teachings they were trying to teach me in certain aspects.

One side of my family was more religious, while the other side was not as much. My biggest struggle in life was trying to figure out who I was. Some people had their visions of how I was supposed to be, while others told me to simply be myself. This internal battle continued from childhood into adulthood. It placed me in a position where I never judged anyone because I had my battles searching for my true path. How could I tell someone else what's best for them when I was still learning myself?

Regardless of my struggles, I was always very sociable and willing to help anyone. Even if it meant simply lending an ear for them to vent, I wouldn't say many knew or even cared about what I was facing. To many, I appeared to be a very strong, smart, and funny kid, often the life of the party. I did experience a lot of jealousy from girls my age because all my friends were guys. Being light-skinned with pretty hair and hanging out with guys wasn't always the best as I got older. I often made people laugh with my jokes, but once I walked away, they would talk about me, saying, "She talks too much," or "Why is she even here?" I just wanted to find a place where I fit in. This desire led me on a journey, seeking love in all the wrong places and from all the wrong people.

Basketball became my passion. I wasn't much for talking about everything I kept bottled up inside. All those secrets felt too heavy to share, so instead, I'd just grab my basketball and head out to the court. Basketball was my first love. I controlled the ball, and the ball did not control me. I would walk up and down the streets, sometimes bouncing the ball gently, other times aggressively. I could run, cry, scream, and no one knew why I was doing it. I put all my focus and emotions on the court. I could be as aggressive as I wanted to be and didn't have to be home. Solitude is what kept me from mentally snapping out on anyone and everyone.

I learned how to go off by myself, think, and figure out how to get away from all the pain I was holding in. I was never a kid who liked to talk about my emotions, maybe because I never really knew how. My voice felt like it was taken at a young age. "What you think doesn't matter" or "I don't care how you feel about this or that" was said often, to the point where I felt like, what's the point of even saying anything? Nobody cares anyway. So, I became a self-made person, some would say. Pain has always been fuel to me. Hurt, disappointments, letdowns— everything made me very hard internally, but I still had a heart of gold. When things got too much, I'd just shut down and go off by myself. Somehow, that made all the crazy stuff going on feel a bit more normal.

My aunt was the one who had my back in the beginning, the one who took me in. Behind all of the support and love my aunt had for me, things were happening in her home that were challenging for any teenager to manage. Her husband was molesting me. This man was the only father figure I had. He taught me about cooking, ironing, and washing—things that parents should teach you. This left me so confused even to this day. We all had so much fun together. He never missed a beat with our family. Family outings, Sunday and Monday family nights, eating out. How can someone do something so bad and good at the same time? What was I supposed to do? This man is the only father figure I had that stuck around and taught me important things I would need in life.

He showed me love through his actions—teaching me life skills, spending time with me, and being a consistent presence in my life. But then, he also hurt me in ways that left deep emotional scars. The confusion this caused in my young mind was overwhelming. How could someone who cared for me, who was there for me, also cause me so much pain? It was like living in two different realities, where the same person could be both a hero and a villain.

As a child, it's hard to process such mixed emotions. On one hand, I felt gratitude and affection for the lessons and attention he gave me. On the other hand, there was fear and betrayal from the hurt he caused. These conflicting feelings created a storm inside me that was difficult to navigate. I struggled to understand how love and pain could come from the same source. It made me question my worth and whether I deserved to be cared for without being hurt. This inner turmoil has stayed with me, shaping my trust in others and my understanding of what family and love means.

Coping with abuse wasn't always easy. There were moments when the emotions were so intense that I felt like the world was going to end. I tried to stay as busy as I could. I worked extra hours, played every sport you could think of, and hung out with my friends. After enduring so much abuse for so long, it became normal to me. Some people may say that I was a young prostitute. I knew he was coming every night whether I wanted him to, so I got ready and just enjoyed it. This woke up my sex drive. I was very self-conscious about my body for years and didn't want to be touched. However, the urge was still there. It was conflictual; my mind was saying no, but my body's urges were crying out and saying yes.

My aunt's husband took advantage of the fact that he had access to me whenever he wanted. There were times when my aunt would send me to give him things or deliver messages to him; he would use those moments to further abuse me. Unfortunately, these experiences created a core belief that no one will ever give you anything for free. I also started to believe that sex was the way that love was communicated, and if no one touched me, then that meant that they did not love me.

When I was 16, the abuse I was suffering was exposed, and that's when I felt like my world, as I once knew it, got turned upside down. My grandmother had passed away, and I was at my oldest sister's house. She had all her friends there, and we were all drinking and smoking. Everyone began to share personal things about themselves. Some of those things were about sex, abuse, trauma, and all sorts of things that no one who was sober would ever just talk about in an open forum. I remember opening my mouth, and before I knew it, I disclosed the abuse that had been happening with my uncle. I quickly tried to retract the statement and asked them not to share it with anyone. Everyone told me that they would keep it to themselves.

Not only was my uncle abusing me, but he was also cheating on my aunt. When she found out about his cheating, we temporarily went to stay with my uncle's family. I remember sitting in the room, and my mother called on the phone. She was so upset that I realized that someone had told her about the abuse that was happening with my uncle. I was so shocked and did not know how to respond. My aunt was sitting there watching me have this conversation with my mother on the phone. After denying it, I quickly hung the phone up. My aunt was not about to let this go. She took that phone and called my mother back, and she discovered the secret I had kept from her for the past eight years.

My aunt and I never really talked about the details of the abuse. She called the police and was told that I had to make the report. I was sixteen at the time, and the last thing I wanted was to report the only man I knew as a father. You see, I came from nothing. When my aunt took me in, I had things that would never have been given to me if I were living with my mother. When I weighed the pros and cons of the situation, there was no way I was going to give up everything I had and possibly risk homelessness. I was willing to pay the price for the lifestyle I had with my aunt. This was also the reason that I never told my aunt when she would often ask me if anyone had ever touched me.

As I said before, my aunt was very spiritual. She had prophetic dreams where God would show her that a man was doing some sexual things that he should not have been doing. Part of me thinks that she knew something was happening but was too scared to investigate it. I am not sure if the rest of my family was informed because no one came to me. There wasn't an embracement, no words of affirmation. It was like things went back to normal, as if nothing had happened. The only difference was that my uncle was no longer living with me.

I began to get rebellious and started walking a different path on my own. I carried so much guilt, shame, hurt, anger, and fear, and these feelings began to intensify. I felt shame and guilt because I felt like I had broken up my aunt's marriage by sleeping with her husband. I was angry that this had happened. Part of me felt nasty and just disgusted. I couldn't tell anyone about these feelings. I couldn't even understand them. I had no idea where my life was headed. There were problems everywhere I turned, and I felt like I was the root cause of all of those problems. I knew I could keep my family as long as I stayed quiet. But the moment someone found out, I would be sent to foster care. I worked a lot to prepare for that possibility and tried to save my money, always ready for whatever might come.

Everything I had started doing went against the morals and values imparted into me. This led my aunt to ask me to leave her home while I was 16. I was on my own for a while until a church member saw me smoking a cigar and told my aunt. The police were called, and I was told I had to return home. I didn't understand because she was the one that kicked me out. So, I returned home.

As life began to happen, I realized that I started to become attracted to females. I remember when I first started dating my ex-girlfriend, we would sit for hours on the phone, talking to each other. We both had endured so much trauma at a young age, and we connected on a much deeper level. For the first time, I had someone I could talk to who truly understood. Her family did family things—the simple things I had always wanted to be a part of. They opened their arms to me, or so I thought. I was just an outsider looking in, not wanting their life but longing for a life of my own where I could connect with a family.

There was this one time I was texting my girlfriend because my aunt was on my case about something else she didn't think I was doing correctly. The text read, "This B★★★H is tripping again." Lo and behold, the message went to my aunt instead of her. She walked out of the gas station, approached me in the back seat, started snapping, went to town on me, kicked me out of the car, and left me there. I was at a shore stop in Greenwood, Delaware, walking down the street. I remember my ear bleeding, cuts on my face, a contact knocked out of one eye. I had no clothes, no money, nothing but the very things I had on me. I was kicked out again at 17, but I was closer to 18 this time. The police told my aunt there was nothing they could do; I was almost 18. So, at 17, I started my journey on my own. I had no family; all I had was me, my girlfriend, and her family. Her mother took me in for a while until she got kicked out, leaving us back at square one, homeless. In my senior year of high school, trying to make a way out of no way with no support.

During this difficult time, I had a teacher who was like an angel to me. I would call her my angel sent from above. She was simply amazing at what she did. I didn't always feel like I was the smartest, and I knew I had many challenges that others didn't, so learning was sometimes hard for me. But from the school's point of view, she never made me feel like I was slow. She always spoke life into me, being that I always heard negativity. She didn't mind putting in extra time for anyone. She was a teacher that took the time to get to know her students. She would know if I was off and knew what was me and what wasn't. That goes a long way in a child's life.

What was so special to me was that I never knew what she was facing in her own life. Why was she always so nice? She gave without a second thought, never looking for something in return, and was genuinely rooting for me to be the best me I could be. She wouldn't let go of my hand even when I wanted to let go of hers. Many people don't get into the rhythm of my heart, but she surely did, wanting nothing in return from me, which was very different for me. I will forever be grateful to this teacher for her words of life that kept me going after what I want in life, regardless of how hard it may be. I know I can do anything I put my mind to.

When I told her what had happened to me, she took me to social services and helped me get a hotel room for 30 days and food stamps. But I still had someone with me that I felt I had to protect; at the time, she was pregnant. So, going to school became harder because I knew if I left my hotel room and housekeeping came in and saw anyone other than myself there, I would be back on the streets. So, I had to choose a place to stay or my education. I dropped out and worked, and we got our first apartment. I didn't see my aunt again until I was 22 years old; by that time, I was pregnant with my first child.

After the sexual trauma that I experienced, I found myself very shy at times and protective of myself. I often thought that people only wanted me around for what I could do or offer them.

I started to associate love with sex. My uncle always said he loved me. He showed his love by providing for my physical needs, but sex was also involved. I started to cling to people who shared similar traumas. More than anything, I craved genuine love, regardless of its form or feeling. I often felt unloved, unwanted, rejected, and abandoned, wondering why a God so highly spoken of by others would allow me to be born into a world where everyone seemed to leave me or give up on me.

My whole understanding of love was messed up. Whenever someone even acted like they were being nice, I thought it was love because I felt different receiving something other than tough love. It was a new feeling for me, one that made me feel seen and cared for, even if only temporarily. But I learned yet again that love doesn't always love me. Abuse and hurt continued to come from people who said, "I love you." This pattern of pain made it difficult to trust and left me questioning whether I would ever find a love that didn't come with strings attached or hidden scars.

In my early 20s, I felt like I was taking control of my life— or so I thought. What I didn't realize was that my past trauma, though no longer occurring, continued to haunt me as I grew older. I was very submissive to my uncle, a behavior I now recognize as a trauma response. Each time he came into my room, I submitted whether I wanted it or not. This response surfaced during a sexual interaction I planned to have with a male. I initially thought I was ready, but then I changed my mind. Unfortunately, he refused to accept my "no" and became very aggressive. The next thing I knew, I was lying on the bed, looking out of the window, crying, as yet another man took my body just because he wanted to.

I had another experience at a "Going Away Party" for one of the guys from the neighborhood. He was turning himself into prison the next day, so he threw a party to celebrate his freedom before being locked up. I was drinking and smoking, and I remember feeling like I needed to rest. I asked my friend if he minded if I laid down, and then I went into the bedroom to lie down. The next thing that I remember was waking up without my clothes on and a man lying on top of me.

Life was so overwhelming that I thought the only way out was to end mine. No matter how much I wished for death or how many times I attempted to end my life, I couldn't shake the feeling that I had to keep going. Deep down, I believed I was meant to make it; I just had to survive. The pain had become my driving force, even to this day. People around me seemed to think I was incredibly strong. Even my mother once said, "I knew you were okay, and I didn't have to worry about you." Because I never wanted to appear weak, I shouldered this thing called life and navigated it as best as I could.

Life was so overwhelming and so far out of my control. There were moments when life just got too much for me. I no longer wanted to live it. I attempted to take my own life multiple times. Each time I tried, God intervened and said, "No". In 2016, after my final suicide attempt, I woke up from a fog and realized where I was. The embarrassment of being rushed to the hospital hit me hard. Despite everything I faced, I knew I had a reason to live. At that moment, I realized I must have a purpose in life and that giving up was not an option. I stood up and left the hospital, determined to find my happiness. I knew my past did not define my future, and I stopped looking for love in others. Instead, I learned how to love myself and the person I saw in the mirror. I believed that everything else would fall into place.

I was always taught that the Bible says to love others as we love ourselves. I took that to heart, hoping that one day I would see that love returned for real. I never want to give up on love because love is what saved me. Despite the hurt and betrayal, I still believe in the power of love. It's what keeps me going, what makes me believe that one day, I'll find the kind of love that doesn't come with strings attached or hidden scars. I know I can do anything I put my mind to, and I hold onto the hope that love will continue to guide me through life's challenges.

I'm no longer an easy target because I know the signs and red flags. I'm very guarded, like an onion with many layers. The more comfortable I become, the more layers I peel back. I started believing in people's actions more than their words because I got tired of getting hurt. All I wanted was to pour out the love I had inside of me, but I never got the chance. I felt like I had to wear a mask to hide who I was because I loved deeply. I knew I was called to love.

I've been through hell and back, but I'm still standing. I knew I would achieve great things from an early age because I believed it in my heart. No matter how dark things got, I always felt a push that wouldn't let me quit. If I kept fighting and kept walking, I knew brighter days would come for me. So, I kept walking. I have yet to find a tunnel without an end. The choice was to turn back or keep going, knowing that the end must be near.

As I reflect on my journey, my aspirations for the future are to become the greatest version of myself and to establish youth centers worldwide, helping children everywhere. Every child deserves a safe place, and I have a deep passion for supporting our youth. I wish I could help every broken child, speak life into them, and encourage them. I envision volunteers showing up to children's games to support them and let them know someone is here for them and with them.

Considering the lessons learned from my past, I plan to achieve these goals by leveraging my experiences of hurt, pain, and disappointment to fuel my drive for greatness. This drive isn't just for the young ones but for all broken people. I desire peace and aim to make a difference in this world, even if it's one person at a time. As a paraprofessional, I am living out part of my passion by helping young children thrive despite the odds they face. The strongest weapon anyone has is belief—believing you can achieve anything you set your mind to.

LETTER TO SELF

Dear Younger Me,

I know the pain you're feeling right now seems unbearable, and the weight of the trauma feels like it may suffocate you. But please know it was not your fault; you did not cause this. The hurt inflicted upon you was unjust and undeserved. You are stronger than your struggle. What you went through is for a greater purpose. I want you to give yourself permission to grow, and all this won't break who you will become if you don't allow it. Stay focused no matter how many times you want to quit; just keep pushing. Every tunnel has an ending, but the only way to get to it is to go through it. It can become very dark, but hold on to God's hands, and for the times you can't feel Him, know He is always with you; just listen to His voice.

You are not responsible for what happened to you. Healing is a journey, so take your time. Feeling the emotions is okay; don't keep running from them. That's what makes you human. Process your emotions and forgive. It's not your weight to carry; it's too heavy for you. Find your truth and live it unapologetically because it costs to become the boss. You are more than a conqueror. Your voice does matter, so use it. You don't have to silence your pain anymore; let it all out so you can get the help you need now. Heal, be free, and spread your wings and fly, baby girl. You are me, and I am you. I give you full permission to heal. You're safe now. I love you, and I am proud of you! You're still here when many didn't make it.

With love, Your Older Self

~ Dametra

CHAPTER FOUR

Here We Grow Again

Patricia Hollingsworth

It was a typical day, waking up and getting ready for school. Often, I felt restless due to countless nights of lack of sleep. Every night, for as long as I can remember, I would have this evil presence that would come to my window and literally stare at me until daybreak. I remember lying in bed with my head covered, leaving just enough of an opening to breathe. My soul would be terrified throughout the night. After several nights of perspiring heavily from the stress of what I was encountering, one day, I got brave enough to peek and look at this presence that came to haunt me. It was the scariest thing I had ever seen in my life. Its color was as dark as midnight, but the most memorable aspect was its yellowish eyes. They had a piercing look as if they could see right through me. It would never talk, just stare at me. I could sense the eeriness that protruded from it. My brothers, who shared a bed, would be sleeping soundly while I, of course, would be wide awake. I would slide down from the top bunk bed and go jump in bed with them, trying my best not to wake them up. Snuggled up between the two, I felt safe and eventually fell asleep. As morning approached and daylight began to come, I remember hearing this presence running away. This would happen every night. There were times when my brothers would wake up and demand that I get out of bed. I never told them what was happening to me because they probably wouldn't have believed me anyway.

I would turn the lights on because that made me feel safe as well, but when my mother got up for her nightly patrol through the house to check on everyone, she would always turn off the lights in our room. Listening intently for her bed to creak, which signaled that she had returned to her bed, I would immediately jump up and flick the light back on. To this day, I do NOT sleep in complete darkness; I have to have some kind of night light or television on to have a peaceful night's sleep. I'm not sure when the evil visitations stopped, but I'm so glad they did! It's ironic how life can take a turn. My brothers were my protectors, especially my oldest brother, and as you will read in this story, the tables turned, and I had to be the one looking out for him.

My story began in the heart of Wilmington, Delaware, on October 1, 1970. Nestled in the middle of two brothers, I found my place in our family dynamic, embodying the role of the middle child with a unique blend of independence and connection. My mother and I weren't always the closest. I was what you might call a tomboy; I was into climbing trees, running barefoot on stones, lifting weights, riding dirt bikes, washing cars and motorcycles, practicing target shooting, etc., not cooking, baking, sewing, or similar activities. So, I wasn't interested when my mom tried to teach me. She had to force me to do those things. She would often compare me to one of my cousins because she loved to do those activities and excelled at them. That used to bother me a lot, and to this day, I hate being compared to someone else. It made me feel like I wasn't good enough, which caused a rift in our relationship and closeness. I always thought, "I am me, and they are them—accept me for who I am, and don't try to change me into who you think I should be ."That was hurtful and made me feel like I wasn't good enough in her eyes. Today, we are closer, but there are times when I still feel like what I do isn't good enough for her. Still, it's not her way of doing things!

My bond with my father was unshakable, earning me the lifelong title of a daddy's girl. One of my greatest joys in life was waiting for my father to come home from a hard day's work. I would run to the car and jump into his arms. He always had a surprise for us. My father worked hard at his place of employment, but he was mostly a hustler. He was always swapping and trading something. He never kept anything for long except his family. He always had something different and exciting for us, whether it was a bike, motorcycle, dirt bike, go-kart, BB gun, boat, car, designer clothes etc. You just never knew; all you knew was that it would be something exciting. I was the only girl, and everyone said I looked just like him. My mother often said that my father would let me get away with things my brothers couldn't.

My childhood is painted with vivid memories, but one Christmas stands out with particular clarity. At the age of six, the excitement of receiving a Big Wheel named Yellow Jacket remains a cherished memory, a symbol of the simple joys of childhood. I still remember the day our parents bought us our Big Wheels—none of the other gifts mattered. I remember looking under the beautiful, shiny silver tree we had for several years and seeing these three large gifts. We raced over to the tree and ripped off the wrapping paper. I remember we all gasped in awe. "Oh wow..." Our father couldn't assemble them fast enough. I remember jumping on my Big Wheel, which I named Yellow Jacket, and pedaling as fast as possible. My brother and I would race all the time when we had free time. I remember running home from the bus stop and hurrying to do our homework so we could ride our Big Wheels. It was the best gift ever.

My grandmother on my father's side was the beacon of the family. It was her faith and her relationship with God that made her stand out. Her hands were literally blessed. Whatever she touched seemed to prosper. She was a wonderful cook and loved doing it. She always had money and was considered the bank of the family, especially by her three grandchildren, who would always go to her for a dollar to buy penny candy. She had a relationship with the store owner that allowed her to write checks and we could get candy. That was when they returned the checks you wrote back to you with your bank statement. My grandmother would have a large stack of returned paid checks with our names on them, where she paid for our candy. My grandmother was a woman of faith and had the gift of healing in her hands. We literally saw miracles happen right before us by the power of God working through her. My baby brother had ringworm in his head, and it was bad. She said, "Bring him to me," and she poured oil on his head and prayed the prayer of faith. Immediately, the ringworm dried up, and his hair began to grow back in that spot. The doctor wanted to hospitalize me because I had pneumonia, and I said, "Mom, Mom, I don't want to stay in the hospital." She prayed for me, and my lungs cleared up. There were no more signs of pneumonia in my lungs when I went back to the doctor. There are so many more stories I could tell you about my grandmother. I could talk to her about anything; she never judged me and always encouraged me.

Our household was a tapestry of relationships and roles. I shared an inseparable bond with my oldest brother, often mirrored in our matching outfits. Our youngest brother was spoiled, of course. My older brother and I were very close. He often protected me by scaring off guys I liked, fearing they would hurt me. In 1987, at the age of 17, he was in a severe car accident that changed his life forever. I remember the day it happened so vividly. It was a day like any other, or so I thought. I went to school, attended classes, and went about my routine, completely unaware that my world was about to be turned upside down. The accident occurred at school, but I was left in the dark. The school didn't tell me a thing. I went through the entire day oblivious to the fact that my brother had been in a severe car accident. It wasn't until a friend of both my brother and me approached me, assuming I already knew, that I was informed. She looked at me with wide eyes, her voice trembling as she said, "I thought you knew."

As I processed the news, I felt like I was feeling all of my thoughts and emotions at the same time. I felt intense anger at the school's negligence. I was numb, in shock, unable to fully comprehend the reality of the situation. It felt unreal, like a bad dream I couldn't wake up from. The thought of seeing my brother in such a critical state scared me beyond words. "My brother shall live and not die," I repeated to myself like a mantra, clinging to hope. I couldn't help but think, "I could have been in the car." Anger surged through me—why hadn't the school notified me? Fear gripped me as I imagined what I might see at the hospital. I was terrified of accidents, hospitals, and wheelchairs. I couldn't understand why my brother hadn't listened to whatever warnings might have prevented this.

My brother's car was totaled. He was hurt very badly and had to be flown in a helicopter to the hospital. The gravity of the situation hit me like a ton of bricks. My mother wasn't there to comfort me; she was at the hospital, where she would remain for four months, staying by my brother's side. I had to face my fears of hospitals and wheelchairs head-on. The possibility of death and losing a sibling ruminated large in my mind. Seeing my brother in a critical state was a distressing experience that forced me to confront my deepest fears.

My brother had to have back surgery, which left him paralyzed from the waist down. Initially, it was thought he had broken his neck, but fortunately, it wasn't broken. However, he had pressure on his brain, and they had to drill into his head to relieve it. He was in a coma for a week. The doctors stressed that the longer he remained in a coma, the worse his chances would be for avoiding brain damage and that he might not come out of it. They allowed family and friends to visit him, hoping we could encourage him to keep fighting even though he was in intensive care.

I was terrified of hospitals and certainly didn't want to see my brother in such a condition, but everyone knew how close we were and stressed that I needed to go. I was terrified; they had to almost push me into the room. When I was pushed into the room, at first, I was overwhelmed and filled with fear and anxiety. I conquered a fear that was deeply embedded in me. For most of my life, I have been an introvert, so instead of internalizing my feelings, I was able to show them and feel safe in doing so.

Once inside, my heart nearly stopped at the sight of all those tubes and machines hooked up to him, but I knew I had to be strong for him. So when I called his name, he responded for the first time; his eyes opened, and tears ran down his face. After seeing his reaction to my voice, there was a sense of peace, relief, reassurance, joy, and hope. I let him know that I was there, that I loved him, and that he had to keep fighting. It was one of the hardest things I've ever had to do, especially at the age of 15.

Shortly after that, he came out of the coma. We give God praise! There is nothing worse than seeing someone you love at death's door, in pain and feeling helpless except to pray. Today, we are close, but not as we once were. My brother has had to deal with a lot, leading him to cope with his trauma in not-so-good ways. The accident and his coping methods have affected our relationship, but we still have each other's back. That will never change. As the protector of the family, I found comfort and expression through writing, pouring my feelings and emotions onto the pages of my tablet.

All my life, I felt like I had to protect others. When I was raped, I protected my two uncles by not telling anyone. I protected my father by keeping silent because he would have physically harmed my uncles, and my grandmother, whose world revolved around her children, would have died of a broken heart. So, I suffered in silence to protect them. I was the protector of my friends, serving as the designated driver when they drank too much. I'm very protective of my family, especially my grandkids, and I was especially protective over my husbands, particularly the last one. I am protective of those I love because I now understand that this is how God made me. He endowed me with endurance and grace, giving me the ability to fight. My fight is through prayer, on my knees. My ability is to see the enemy from afar and intercede before he gets too close to me or the ones I love. To sound the alarm when trouble is coming and to provide strategies for defeating the enemy of our souls. It is to be a shield for those who cannot fight for themselves but also to teach them how to fight in the Spirit and in the natural, for we do not wrestle against flesh and blood but against principalities, powers, rulers of the darkness, and spiritual wickedness in high places. There is a war going on out here, and we must know how to fight, starting with the mind first. As a man thinks, so is he. I have a strong personality; many don't understand me, but that's okay. I know my role in life, and I'm comfortable with who I am. I'm the type of person who prays before making a decision, but once God speaks and I make up my mind to do something, it's set in stone; there's no stopping me!

Solitude was a friend, and my walks down the long road we lived on became sacred moments of conversation with God. These walks, alongside the sanctuary of my makeshift tree house, were my refuge, a place where I could be myself and reflect. My treehouse had materials that served as curtains. I kept my little teacups and pot there for tea parties with my doll. An old towel served as a rug for us to sit on. It was a peaceful place for me, and occasionally, one of my friends would come over. We would sit in the treehouse together, pretending we were cooking. Even as a kid, I did a lot of reflecting on life there.

My prayer life, even from a young age, has helped me identify where the enemy lies and waits, trying to deceive whoever he can. It has enabled me to recognize the struggles I have faced and overcome 'and to see those same struggles in others. It has inspired me to be a beacon of light for others and to choose compassion over judgment. When it comes to relationships, it has been challenging because many have been one-sided. The love I have given hasn't always been reciprocated, as many didn't know how to love me in the way I needed or wanted. As a result, I expended a lot of energy, often feeling depleted. A car can only run on fumes for so long before running out of gas. I had to reevaluate whom I was entering into relationships with and see if they had the capacity to support me when I needed it.

My grandmother's presence was a source of strength; her tranquility and my writings became my pillars, supporting me through the complexities of growing up. Family time was sacred, especially during the summer. Our father's commitment to weekend fishing trips from dawn till dusk or visits to the race tracks instilled in us the value of togetherness and mutual care. The principle of sharing was ingrained in us, fostering a culture of collective well-being within our family.

High school brought new responsibilities, and I naturally assumed the role of caretaker, ensuring my friends' safety as the designated driver during dances and after parties. Choosing orange juice over alcohol, I abstained from drinking and smoking, a choice that became a humorous quirk among my peers. However, standing out never phased me. The courage to be different, to stand alone if necessary, was a trait I carried with pride. This mindset, a testament to the values and experiences that shaped me from childhood in Wilmington to who I am today, allowed me to embrace my uniqueness without hesitation.

Being the designated driver and steadfast in my decision to be myself and dare to be different earned me the label of the responsible one. Yet, to some, it also painted me as someone who thought she was better than everyone else—a misconception far from the truth. I simply didn't see the appeal in drinking, dealing with hangovers, vomiting over a toilet bowl, and being unaware of my surroundings. Moreover, after experiencing rape, staying alert and aware at all times became even more critical for me.

I've had my share of trauma and have learned a lot about myself as I went through it. When I was about 5 or 6, I had a scary moment that's etched in my memory forever—I fell out of a moving car. Somehow, I ended up sitting in the middle of the road, watching our car drive away. They didn't realize I was gone until they were pretty far down the road. Looking back, considering how fast the car was going, I was incredibly blessed not to be hurt. I remember feeling frozen in place, just waiting for someone to realize and come back for me. When I finally got back in the car, I was so shaken that I couldn't even talk for a long time.

As if falling out of a car wasn't traumatic enough, I had another incident involving a car when I was 7. My brothers and I were playing; they were tickling me, and in all the chaos, I ended up hitting my head on a car rim my dad had left inside. It was bad—I had a huge cut, but we never went to the hospital. My mom and grandma took care of it until it healed up. Nowadays, I deal with migraines and eye problems, and sometimes, I can't help but wonder if that fall has something to do with it.

As I progressed in life, it seemed like trauma followed me. I faced sexual abuse from within my own family, starting at age eight and not stopping until I was 15. At 16, things took a bit of a turn for the better when I met my son's dad, my first serious love. I became pregnant at 16 and a mom at 17. I was a mom, and it felt like maybe things were looking up. At age 20, I was filled with hope as my son's father, and I built a house from the ground up. We meticulously chose every detail, from the light fixtures to the shutters. But just two years later, at age 22, I discovered him—my first love and fiancé—cheating. Heartbroken, I packed up and left, abandoning the dream home we had created together. In retrospect, walking away from that house was a decision I would come to regret; it sat empty and lifeless for two years after I moved out.

That same year, I found comfort and strength by embracing faith and forging a personal relationship with God, which became a crucial anchor in my life. By 23, I was married. The time leading up to our wedding was a rollercoaster, influenced by the opinions of others, but we held firm to our faith and plans. Marrying him was one of the best decisions I ever made, though our union eventually dissolved after 12 years due to his infidelity, plunging me into despair once more.

The year 2003 was challenging for me. My grandmother, my best friend, and the family's rock, passed away from cancer. Her wisdom and strength had been a guiding light in my life, and her loss left a void in my heart. I needed time to work through the grief and loss of such a matriarch within our family. Then, in January 2006, I discovered my husband was having an affair. I was devastated. I could not believe that this was happening yet again. His infidelity led to our separation and the loss of everything I had—home, car, and sense of security. The emotional toll was immense; I was engulfed in depression, lost 66 pounds, and felt overwhelmed by despair.

About one month later, my father went into the hospital for a routine surgery that went terribly wrong, resulting in severe complications and a two-month hospital stay. Those months were fraught with anxiety and helplessness. Despite the challenges, there were moments of pride and joy too. In June

2006, my son graduated from high school—an event that, despite its costs, was my proudest moment as a parent. He left for college on August 25, 2006, marking a hopeful milestone. The challenging year finally drew to a close when my divorce was finalized on October 2, 2006. On October 8, 2006, I went on a date with someone who wasn't my usual type, hoping to try something new. Unfortunately, it was a poor decision—I ended up pregnant by him, and he turned out to be bad news.

On November 12, 2006, I awoke to excruciating pain in my stomach, the worst I had ever felt. I was nauseous and felt an urgent need to use the bathroom. While sitting on the commode, I became clammy and nearly passed out. Resting my face against the cool bathroom tile provided some relief as I called out to Jesus. Eventually, the pain subsided enough for me to clean up and head to the hospital. Unable to wake my niece with my weakened voice, I threw a shoe into her room to get her attention. She quickly helped me dress, and we rushed to the hospital.

That day nearly became my last. I was unknowingly pregnant in the fallopian tubes, and one had ruptured, causing severe internal bleeding. At the hospital, emergency surgery was necessary. The doctors struggled to find a blood match due to my rare blood type and warned me I had a high chance of not surviving. Miraculously, I made it through without a transfusion, treated only with iron pills for the blood loss. In a desperate plea, I asked the doctors to save the baby, having waited 17 years to become pregnant again, but it was impossible—the tube had ruptured, and the pregnancy was not viable.

By December 20, 2006, my life had taken a positive turn when I met an incredible man, and this led to my marriage in 2007. Our connection was electric, and we quickly found a church we liked. However, it soon emerged that the pastor was a warlock, and his actions undermined our marriage. Still healing from past wounds and operating out of pain, I ended up cheating on him, which led to mistrust that eventually destroyed our relationship. We separated, and he filed for divorce.

By age 37, the divorce was final, leaving me devastated by my actions. Shortly after, I met another man. There was an instant connection, and within weeks, I felt God revealing His purpose for my life with this man. We started a relationship. At age 41, I married again. This relationship, though, proved to be fraught with challenges. It was a domestic violence situation marked by his infidelity. Despite the hardships, our relationship lasted 11 and a half years, with eight of those years spent in marriage.

At age 43, I discovered I was pregnant. Ecstatic about the news, my joy turned to dismay when my husband's immediate concern was the reaction of his other women. Despite our spiritual mother's advice to keep the pregnancy under wraps until after the first trimester, he told his mother—who was not fond of me. Tragically, just four days later, I miscarried. We eventually purchased a home together, though he never truly made it feel like it was mine. About eight months after the purchase, he fell ill, and we faced a barrage of health issues. During a routine EKG for pains that he was having in his legs, doctors discovered an active heart attack. They conducted four EKGs to confirm their findings. At the hospital, alongside his back issues and frequent falls, we also learned about his severe heart condition and uncontrolled diabetes. His recovery from back surgery took a year and a half, during which he couldn't return to work. We drained our savings covering medical costs and maintaining his medication. The strain led to tensions, and despite having previously stopped, he began to be physically abusive again. At that point, I received a stark vision from God about a potentially tragic outcome if I stayed. It was a clear sign I needed to leave. Yet again, after rebuilding and gaining back everything I lost in a previous marriage, I left my husband and our home, filed for divorce in 2018, and it was finalized in 2019.

I've been enjoying my single life from ages 48 to 53 (2019 to 2024). While I'm open to another relationship that could lead to marriage, I'm no longer willing to settle. It's my time to thrive and truly live. I am content and embracing the best phase of my life. I often dream of a future with a man where we are blessed and happy. Until then, I am celebrating myself, engaging in the ministry God has called me to, and continuing to love myself and those He brings into my path. I'm committed to maintaining my peace and wholeness, learning from my past mistakes, and using my experiences to help others avoid similar pitfalls or find healing. My past trauma shapes my story, but my story is ultimately for His glory. God has brought me through it all.

LETTER TO SELF

Dear Patricia,

Recite these affirmations each day:

"I am enough.
I trust the process of life.
I embrace the beauty of my healing.
I am grateful for my strength and courage.
I breathe in calmness and breathe out tension.
My scars are a testament to my strength.
I am deserving of all the good things life has to offer.
I choose to focus on what I can control.
I am a warrior, not a victim."

As I look in the rearview mirror and reflect on my life from an adult perspective, I see a beautiful little girl full of ambition and life. Like many children, I took everyone at face value. In hindsight, I realize that this innocence contributed to many of the challenges I faced later in life. When you have a pure heart, you tend to see others as pure as well—but when reality hits, it can be devastating. I remember thinking, "How did I not see this?" My young mind was naïve and lacked the maturity to recognize the complexities of the world. The Bible says in Titus 1:15: "To the pure, all things are pure, but to those who are corrupted and do not believe, nothing is pure. In fact, both their minds and consciences are corrupted." The innocent are often preyed upon by the wicked, which is why we need good parents and shepherds who fear the Lord to teach, protect, and guide us through the dangers of this world.

That being said, despite our best defenses, sometimes the fox still gets into the henhouse and takes what is precious. This is what has happened to many, and now we are left to deal with the traumas of our lives. Out of fear, I chose not to share my trauma with anyone as a child, believing I could handle it on my own. Now I understand that this was the wrong decision—that the burden was too much for any child my age to carry alone. Deep down, I hoped someone, particularly my mother, would notice my pain. When that didn't happen, it brought a new level of sadness and disappointment. Consciously, I knew she didn't know about the abuse.

Patricia, by all human logic, you have just cause not to forgive or trust anyone because of what you've been through. But I have learned through the help of the Holy Spirit that true freedom comes from reaching beyond our limitations and leaning on the Lord. We must allow Him to reopen the parts of our minds and hearts that have shut down. It's like a car stuck in neutral. Don't let what others have done to you change the condition of your heart. Don't allow the brilliant mind God has given you to be limited in its functioning. You didn't have the tools or the understanding back then, but you do now. Your young, developing mind did what it thought was necessary at the time. I don't blame you—in fact, I applaud your courageous act. You took on what seemed like the weight of the world and did it with a smile.

Patricia, your strengths have supported so many others and have become a way of life for you to this day. But remember this: Know your limitations. Know when to release some people from your life, when to say no, and who is your true assignment. Most importantly, take everyone and everything to the altar, giving them to God. When you feel overwhelmed, run to the Rock that is higher than you—Jesus. Never lose yourself trying to be a people pleaser or trying to be everything to everyone. You've come a long way, and many rely on you for different reasons, which can be burdensome at times. Always remember to point them to God, for He is truly our strength.

Lovingly submitted,

~ Patricia

CHAPTER FIVE

The Beginning And
The End Of My Journey

Deborah Jackson

The beginning of every journey should start with agreement. Unfortunately, my life was a jigsaw puzzle with missing pieces, and every piece I found seemed to reveal even more gaps. Growing up in my family was difficult. My parents argued a lot, and family dinners often ended in disaster. My stepdad took care of me, while my relationship with my mom remained distant. It wasn't until much later that I discovered I had five sisters and that my biological father was someone I unknowingly saw regularly at church. This is the story of my life, filled with family secrets, unexpected kindnesses, and the strength I found to navigate through it all.

I was born in Queens, New York. Soon after, life took a twist when my mother got married, and we moved to Flushing, New York. That's where my younger brother was born in 1970. Honestly, growing up in Flushing wasn't exactly a walk in the park. When I reflect on my early days, my memory's kinda fuzzy around when I was 5. But I do remember my parents arguing a lot. Family dinners? More like a recipe for disaster. Every time they had a few drinks, you could bet something would go wrong. One of my biggest shocks was when I discovered I had five sisters.

This revelation was like a bombshell. I had spent my childhood thinking it was just me and my brother, and suddenly, my understanding of my family was turned upside down. It was confusing and heartbreaking to realize how much had been kept from me. The discovery added another layer of complexity to my already chaotic childhood, leaving me feeling a little angry and sad over the lost time I could have spent getting to know the rest of my family.

Some of my first clear memories are from Flushing. For example, on my mom's wedding day, I had to stay with my Aunt Mae. Things weren't great there, either; my aunt and uncle would fight a lot, usually because he drank too much and would start yelling over nothing. My cousin and I would sit in the living room, trying to tune it out and just laugh to keep from feeling too bad about it all. We were just kids, barely understanding any of the craziness going on around us.

Aunt Mae used to take me to church, a place where, unbeknownst to me, my biological father also attended. The church visits with Aunt Mae was supposed to be a place of comfort, yet I was unknowingly crossing paths with a man who was my father. The secrecy surrounding his identity added layers of confusion and hurt. At that time, I had no idea he was my dad, and I was also unaware that I had sisters. There was a sort of silent agreement among the adults in my life – my grandparents, my mom's sister, her husband, and Aunt Mae – that I shouldn't be told about him. Despite what my mom had said, Aunt Mae didn't follow that rule. Even though I was in the dark about his identity, my dad, his wife, and my sister knew who I was. Visits to my aunt's house often meant running into them since my uncle was their uncle, too.

My mother never wanted me to know who my father was. She had lied to me about his identity. Aunt Mae had been making sure my dad could see me, a gesture of care that meant the world, especially since my mom didn't want him involved in my life. Aunt Mae even went as far as to tell him where I worked when I was 17. By then, I had stopped attending church, which meant I didn't see him anymore, but he kept inquiring about me. I worked at a shoe store in Green Acres Mall, where he occasionally bought shoes during my shifts. Each time, after making a purchase, I'd go to the back to put the other shoes away, only to return and find out from my boss that the man had left an envelope for me. Inside, there was always cash. This was strange to me.

I told my grandma about the man who bought shoes and left an envelope full of money. She didn't say much when I described him, but my grandfather gave her a look that said it all – keep quiet. She did, suggesting maybe it was just a family member trying to give me a little extra. I was so confused but also kinda happy. I mean, who wouldn't be happy to get extra cash? It felt weird, though, like there was this secret everyone knew except me. Each time that man came back to my job, it felt like an odd mix of excitement and mystery. Once, he even brought his daughters with him. I had no idea at the time that they were my sisters. It was like living in a mystery novel where every new chapter added more twists. I didn't know what to think, but I couldn't deny that the extra money was a relief. Feeling grateful to someone I barely knew while feeling this nagging sense of something wrong was strange.

Most of my childhood memories aren't great; they make me feel pretty sad. I always wondered why my family was so mean to each other. It was a different vibe when I'd go over to my mom's sister's place. They'd eat together like a real family.

She was the coolest aunt — she would do my hair because my mom couldn't figure it out, so she let her keep it neat. My family, especially on my mom's side, had its ups and downs. My childhood was filled with loud arguments and too much drama. But there were good times, too. Family BBQs at my grandma's place were like a breath of fresh air. My grandmother was a no-nonsense type of person, and she didn't allow any drama at her place. People respected her and knew she meant business. Those gatherings were peaceful, and for a little while, we felt like a normal family. We also had card nights every Friday at a different family member's house, which brought a sense of routine and connection. My cousin and I were super close; we did everything together. We shared secrets, dreams, and endless laughter. Moving to Queens Village in 1971 was a big change. My cousin went to Brooklyn, and our bond was tested by distance. As for my real dad, I still hadn't met him yet.

So many things were happening in my life that no one knew about. Looking back, I see my parents didn't catch on to the small ways I was changing. We'd have these big family BBQs with my mom's side and my stepdad's side of the family. His nephew and their mom would come over, and his nephew would molest me. I was just 9, and when they visited, I dreaded it. I never told my mom because I feared what they said they'd do if I spoke up. Plus, my parents were usually too drunk to notice anything. How did I deal with all that? I just tried to block it out and pretend it wasn't happening. If I didn't see them, I figured I'd be okay. The one person who was there for me was my best friend, who lived across the street. I never told anyone what was happening to me, not even my aunt, and I felt like I could tell her anything. But this? It just seemed too hard to share.

My mother and I were not exactly close. My stepdad took care of me from when I was about five until I moved in with my grandparents. Moving in with my grandparents provided some stability, but the thought of my unknown biological father always lingered in my mind. Back in the '70s, I had no clue about my real dad. When I moved in with my grandparents, I started to learn what values really meant. My mom never talked about that stuff. My grandma cared about how I presented myself and made sure I finished school. She always said, "There's no such word as 'can't.'" She didn't care what you wanted to be - if you wanted to be a stripper, she'd say, "Be the best stripper you can be." "Be the best you can be" was a phrase I grew up hearing from my grandma, especially to her grandkids. Growing up in the 70s was a whole different ball game; I saw a lot, heard a lot, and went through a lot. Making it to adulthood in New York meant you had to be tough and smart. You were either going to school and carving out a path for yourself or getting caught up in the fast life, like dealing with drug dealers, which could easily derail your life. I learned that the hard way, and it took me until my 30s to start listening to what my grandma had been saying all along.

My grandmother was meticulous about keeping her house spotless, a trait I admired deeply. No matter how much of a handful my grandfather could be, she never turned him away or treated him differently. From her, I learned the importance of personal hygiene and how to maintain a clean home. I suppose that's why my kids jokingly say I have OCD—apparently, I've got a bit of a cleaning disorder. The values she instilled in me have deeply influenced how I raise my kids, teaching them to strive to be the best in whatever path they choose. My perspective on life has significantly evolved; I've learned the importance of saving money and managing my affairs more wisely.

Being a teenager was all about chilling with my crew and trying stuff like smoking weed. I had four main friends, and we're still super tight. I loved hanging at one friend's place because their folks were chill. They'd give us advice about school and jobs and remind us to be picky about our friends. We had a blast going to house parties, block parties and playing handball. Just being with my friends on the block was the best. What made those days special was having friends who always had your back and parents who taught us right from wrong, not just to their kids but to all of us. It's pretty cool to look back and see how we've all grown up and made something of ourselves. We'd always hang out at each other's places, and our parents knew each other well. Things got real when one of us got pregnant and kept it a secret. Suddenly, she wasn't around anymore because her mom, who was super into her church, wouldn't let her out. Then their house caught fire because of all the candles her mom was burning, and I hadn't seen her for about two years.

After those two years, I bumped into her in Ozone Park, and she had a little baby with her. Turns out, she had a baby and was scared to tell us because of how people would talk, especially since she was only 13 and her mom was known in the church. Back then, people were quick to judge. That whole situation taught us to be open with each other; we promised no more secrets. Despite everything, she's doing awesome now and has four kids. That experience showed us how important it is to stick together and be there for each other.

I loved growing up with my grandmother. She knew what it all meant to be a teenager and allowed me to explore myself and test boundaries. She passed away when I was 25 years old. Losing my grandmother was one of the most painful experiences of my life. She wasn't just my grandmother; she was my rock, mentor, and the mother figure I leaned on for guidance, support, and unconditional love. Our relationship was incredibly close; she taught me everything I needed to know about being a woman. Her wisdom and nurturing presence were foundational in shaping who I am today.

When she died, it felt like my world was falling apart. Her stability and reassurance were suddenly gone, leaving me feeling vulnerable. The depth of my relationship with her meant that her loss wasn't just about missing her physical presence but also about the absence of her wisdom, her comfort, and the irreplaceable bond we shared. Her death brought a cascade of emotions—grief, sadness, confusion, and even a sense of abandonment. It was as if the ground beneath me had crumbled, leaving everything chaotic and unsteady. The void she left behind was not just a space; it was a gaping hole.

Her funeral service was held in South Carolina during the summer. After the service, we all gathered in my uncle's yard – my grandpa, aunts, uncles, cousins, and other family members were there. My son, who was just seven months old, stayed inside with my mom. Now, my dad, who I hadn't recognized as my dad at that point, heard about my grandma's passing. Grandma Eva Lou was his mom, so he came to Clark Hill to be with his family. I remember stepping out into the yard, where everyone was laughing and catching up. And there was my dad, a stranger to me, asking if I knew who he was. I was completely taken aback when he said he was my dad. I looked over at my grandpa sitting in the van we'd driven from New York, and he just nodded. My mom's sister confirmed it with a nod, too. I was shocked and ran back to tell my mom what happened. She was furious, storming out to confront him, while my grandpa insisted it was time I knew the truth.

My dad gave me his number, asking me to call him when I got back to New York. He lived in Hempstead, Long Island, New York. I also found out that my father worked for the ATM train, which was right around the corner from where I lived in Bricktown, New York. I cried because I couldn't believe he was so close to me all that time. That 14-hour ride back was painfully silent. Meeting my dad for the first time was shocking and awkward. My mom was especially unhappy about it. She warned me not to talk about her to him and would get upset if my kids teased her about him. Despite her feelings, I grew closer to my dad and his side of the family over time. As years passed, my mom softened a bit, even inquiring about him when he fell ill, although she remained silent about his wife due to the circumstances of my birth. I've felt welcomed by my dad's side of the family. They knew about me, so there was no awkwardness. I've become especially close to his sister and brother.

Holding such a significant secret from a child can be deeply traumatic, and I experienced this firsthand. My sense of identity was closely tied to my family background, and knowing who my parents were was fundamental to understanding who I was. With this information hidden from me, I always felt a sense of incompleteness and confusion about my identity. Discovering that such an important truth had been hidden from me led to significant trust issues. I felt that my family had deceived me, which shattered my trust in not only my family members but also in other relationships.

The secrecy caused considerable emotional distress. I felt a deep sense of betrayal, especially since the truth came out during a moment of vulnerability after losing my grandmother. I was left dealing with grief, sadness, confusion, and even a sense of abandonment because my rock was gone. This news about my father complicated my grieving process, making it harder to cope with both the loss of my grandmother and the shock of meeting my father. I didn't understand why this was so significant that my family had to swear to secrecy to keep it from me. I also didn't understand why it took me losing someone I loved to unlock the sworn bond of secrecy about someone who loved me and whom I could now get to know and love.

My story reached a critical point in 2023 with the passing of my mom. This loss was massive because it meant that all the pain and struggles I went through would never be understood or shared with her. Her death closed the door on any chance of fixing things or making sense of the past together. The journey of dealing with betrayal, discovering hard truths, and facing loss was something I had to go through on my own.

When my mother became sick, I had to make sure her needs were met, which is ironic because she had never cared for me. Now, I was in the role of a mom, nurturing her and ensuring all her needs were met. I often went back and forth to New York from Delaware, managing her care. I never thought about being mad at her; I felt it was a duty and responsibility because although she was never a mother to me, I was still her daughter. I felt a sense of obligation to be present for her during these difficult moments.

When I first learned about my mother's passing, I felt emotions I'd never felt before. The most difficult part about it was that I felt them all at one time. I had gone to see her before she passed away after getting a call from a close family friend. My son got a similar call from his godmother about his grandma. It was confusing because the doctors kept telling me she was fine, but it turned out she wasn't. My son and I went to New York the next day. When we got there, she didn't look the same, and at first, she didn't know who we were. I called my brother so he could talk to her. He reassured her that he had a job and she didn't need to worry about him. She always worried about him. He told her he loved her and promised to see her soon since he had moved to Virginia. I told her I loved her and kissed her forehead, knowing deep down that she would leave us soon. Two days later, it happened.

That day was overwhelming. The doctor called every hour, asking for my permission to revive her after she stopped breathing three times. I eventually told them to stop and let her go, as she had requested. When I got the final call, I was at work. I yelled at the doctor over the phone, "No!" My daughter rushed downstairs, asking what had happened. I told her that Grandma had passed. The reality hit me hard. Now, I had to take care of the things she wanted me to do. My eldest daughter and I went to New York the next day to view her body. Seeing her like that was devastating; no one is ever prepared for that.

Caring for my mother, despite her not having cared for me, was an empowering experience. Stepping into a nurturing role for her felt natural, even though our past was difficult. I never harbored anger towards her; instead, I felt a deep sense of responsibility. This was my way of upholding what I believed was right, regardless of how she had treated me. The process required a lot of emotional strength. Each time she needed resuscitation, it was a battle between hope and reality. Making the decision to let her go after the third time was heart-wrenching, but I knew it was a compassionate choice. I couldn't bear to see her suffer any longer.

98

Through it all, I found that my capacity for compassion and forgiveness was greater than I had imagined. Taking care of her was not just about duty; it was about ensuring she left this world with some dignity and love. This experience taught me that true strength lies in our ability to care for others, even when they haven't done the same for us. Reflecting on my relationship with my mom, it wasn't the greatest. Towards the end, it was different. She was often unhappy with how I managed my family and upset that she hadn't read the first book I wrote. She kept asking my cousin about it. I told her she could read it when she got better and came home because I didn't want her blood pressure to rise over its contents. Her death felt more like losing a family member than losing a mom, probably because my grandmother raised me, and my bond with her was stronger. Nonetheless, I loved my mother because she was my mother.

There were specific unresolved issues that came up when she passed. I was waiting for the perfect time to sit down and share my chapter with her. We never got to read the book together. I couldn't ask her if she knew her nephew had sexually abused me or why she never checked on me when I was the only girl surrounded by boys at night. I also never got to ask her why she didn't want me to know about my real dad and instead chose a man I didn't know. I often wonder how she would feel if she knew all the things I went through and had to live with for years.

The experiences I had with my mother influenced how I raised my kids. I was very strict, always wanting to know who they were with, where they were, and what they were doing. I might have been a pain in their eyes, but I believed I was protecting them. Unlike my relationship with my mom, communication with my kids is open and honest. They talk to me about everything, trying not to hurt my feelings but being truthful. The relationship I have with my children is opposite to the relationship I had with my mother. I wanted to be intentional about breaking cycles and patterns that were passed down in my family from generation to generation.

My relationship with my mother impacted how I interacted with others. I often felt like people wanted something from me, and I took on the role of being there for everyone. My husband calls me "Mother Theresa" because I'm always trying to help someone. With my children, I try to be there no matter what. When they were young, they probably thought I was a pain, always in their business. Even now, they might say I'm still involved, but they know I care. I'm very close to my seven children and their partners, much closer than I was with my mother.

Understanding my feelings towards my mother is complicated. Some family members get it, while others don't. My kids might understand some of what I've been through, but not all. I realize I've been holding back many things about how she treated my kids and me. My family supports me by listening, and I hope they can live their lives better than I did.

There are aspects of my relationship with my mother that I wish to leave behind. One of those is the way she felt about my husband. When she found out I was having a baby with him, she was so upset. She told me, "If you have another baby with that man, he's going to leave you." I can still hear her saying that.

Meanwhile, we've been together for 30 years now. If I could have one last conversation with my mother, I would ask her why she never told me who my real dad was. Did he do something, or did she just feel guilty about how I was conceived? I would feel better knowing the reason. Healing over this is puzzling because I wonder how different my life would have been if I had known my father.

Thinking about these unresolved issues stirs up a mix of emotions. A part of me feels hurt and angry for the secrets she kept, but there's also a part of me that longs to understand her decisions. I wish I could have had the chance to talk to her openly, to ask her the questions that have haunted me for so long.

My mother's decision to stop me from knowing my father was wrong. This significant piece of information she withheld drastically changed the relationship she had. I can't stand a liar! She was now the liar that I couldn't stand! Maybe she did what she thought was right, not knowing how it would affect my life. It turns out to be bittersweet. My grieving process has been confusing. Sometimes, I miss her, and other times, I question why I don't. I wasn't overcome with emotion and tears as I had been with my grandmother's passing. Instead, there was a strange numbness, accompanied by a sense of shame for not mourning my mother in the same way. Is it because we weren't close or because my grandparents raised me? My feelings are all over the place. I began to wonder if my feelings were more about mourning the lost potential of a relationship rather than the actual loss of my mother. There were so many unresolved issues and unanswered questions between us. I grieved not just for her death but for the relationship we never had and the secrets that kept us apart. Understanding this complexity has been a challenging but essential part of my healing journey. I did love her as my mother. Our relationship was different, and I always respected her. Whatever she asked me to do, I did it. I have no regrets about being her daughter.

Finding peace and forgiveness in my relationship with my mother has been a journey. Finding peace and forgiveness in my relationship with my mother has been a journey filled with ups and downs. When I first found out the truth about my father, I felt a strong sense of anger and betrayal. Learning this secret made me feel like my mother had kept a big part of my life hidden from me. This discovery was painful and added to the emotional distance between us.

As I navigated through my grief and confusion after her passing, I realized that holding on to resentment would only hinder my healing. I began to seek understanding and empathy, trying to piece together the reasons behind my mother's choices. Was she protecting me, or was she unable to confront her past? These questions haunted me, but they also helped me to see things from a different perspective. Forgiving my mother didn't mean I was okay with what she did or that the pain was gone. It meant I was letting go of the anger that kept me stuck in the past. It was about accepting that our relationship was complicated and that holding onto resentment wasn't helping me move forward. Finding peace meant accepting that my relationship with my mother was far from perfect. It meant grieving for the relationship we never had and the secrets that kept us apart. Through this acceptance, I began to heal.

Despite everything she did, I followed her wishes on how she wanted to go. She always said to make sure she was laid to rest with her mom in Clark Hill, South Carolina. I made sure of that with the help of my cousin. After processing everything she did, I felt in my heart that I would have to forgive her for peace. Honoring my mother means being my best mother, wife, sister, and grandmother. On Mother's Day 2024, my son wrote to me in the family chat, "Love you more, Mom. Lord knows you get on my nerves from time to time being extra nosey, lol, but the love you have for us—I wouldn't trade it for the world. You truly are a great mother. Wouldn't know what to do without you; you always have our backs, right or wrong. Again, love you." That message shows my closeness to my kids, even if I get on their nerves. There's no way I could have talked to my mother like that out of respect. Times have changed, and it's important to communicate with your children so they can express how they feel without fear of being shut down.

I've made it a priority to be open and honest with my own family, breaking the cycle of secrecy and mistrust. In doing so, I hope to create a legacy of love and understanding that honors the best parts of my mother's memory while leaving behind the painful aspects of our relationship. The journey to peace and forgiveness is ongoing. It has its ups and downs, just like my memories and grief. But with each day, I feel more at peace with my past, more able to forgive the flaws in our relationship, and more thankful for the lessons I've learned along the way.

Reflecting on "The Beginning and End of My Journey," I realize how far I've come in understanding and processing my relationship with my mother. The road has been filled with moments of pain, confusion, growth, and healing. By addressing the unresolved issues and embracing open communication, I've learned to honor my mother in a way that brings peace to my heart.

My journey isn't just about the past; it's about how I choose to move forward. I've turned the lessons from my childhood into a commitment to be a better mother, wife, sister, and grandmother. I've embraced the values of love, honesty, and support, creating a family environment where my children can freely express themselves and know they are unconditionally loved. As I continue to navigate this journey, I find comfort in the love and bonds I've built with my family. The beginning of my journey was marked by secrecy and unanswered questions, but the end is defined by understanding, forgiveness, and the constant support of those closest to me. This chapter of my life has come full circle, and I am grateful for the lessons I learned along the way.

LETTER TO SELF

Dear Younger Me,

As I sit here reflecting on our journey, I think about all the trauma we've been through. The pain was immense and overwhelming at times. We tried to convince ourselves that none of it existed, but that only made things harder. We locked these painful memories away, calling them our "inmates." I often wondered why we weren't allowed to know who our dad was and why the changes happening in our lives went unnoticed. I want you to know that it wasn't Mom's fault; she simply didn't know better. Understanding this has been a key step in our healing process.

Our relationship with Mom seems broken, strained, and sometimes nonexistent. It often feels like she doesn't even act like our mom. But I want you to know that through the pain we experienced as a child, purpose blossomed, and invaluable lessons of wisdom emerged that we wouldn't have gained otherwise. We learned to always listen to our children and encourage them to speak their minds. We also learned to think before we speak because our words can be like razor blades, cutting through the soul and self-worth of another person. On this journey, we also learned to forgive those who caused us trauma. This forgiveness has been a cornerstone of our emotional resilience.

It's important to permit yourself to grow past everything that has happened to you. Our past doesn't define us, and we are much stronger than the struggles we've experienced. Keep this in mind because this realization will make us a stronger person. The weight of our past has lifted, and we embrace the healing process. We've made it through the trauma; it hasn't taken over our lives but has instead made us stronger. We've learned to see life's beauty and be grateful for our strength in this healing journey. We are free of all our trauma, and we let God take it into His hands. Embracing faith has given us the courage to move forward with hope and optimism.

With all my love,

~ Deborah

CHAPTER SIX

Somewhere To Belong

Michelle Jones

It was a regular day in San Diego—sunny and warm. Playing outside without parents was the norm as a 7-year-old in the early '80s. My sisters and I felt safe at the park. We came home laughing and smiling, typical for children with seemingly perfect, happy lives. However, this day would later reveal itself to be a turning point, shaping my brain for a lifetime of turmoil and struggle with borderline personality disorder (BPD). It impacted my thoughts, feelings of self-worth, and my intense desire to belong. To fit in somewhere, I found myself willing to do anything.

My story details the lengths I went to and the suffering I endured in my quest for belonging, to avoid abandonment, and to escape the constant feeling of wanting to die. That sunny day in San Diego marked the beginning of my internal struggle when I no longer felt I belonged to anyone. It all started with the shock of thinking my father had killed my mother.

I was born in Dover, Delaware, but I don't remember anything from those early days. My real story starts in San Diego, which was pretty much my world until sixth grade. After that, my life turned into a back-and-forth between San Diego and Dover, as I lived in two places simultaneously. It was like this constant shuffle became the theme of my childhood, a mix of new sights and a whirlwind of feelings. My siblings were my silver lining. My brother, a decade my junior, was (and still is) a source of pure joy. My sisters, each in their way, added color and comfort to my life. Despite the distances and the comings and goings, the bonds we formed were my lifeline, my sanity amidst the chaos. I've got three siblings from my dad's side, and technically, there are more out there, but they're strangers to me. Then, there's the sister who's entirely mine, sharing both parents with me, and a brother from my mom. In my family, we don't use the term "half" – to us, we're just brothers and sisters. I'm the oldest kid my mom has.

As the older sister, I never felt burdened with extra responsibilities. I didn't have to look after the younger ones— that was their mothers' job. I wasn't an automatic babysitter. My childhood was split between two families, each with its distinct atmosphere. However, I want to talk about my time with my mother, sister, and brother. I cherished being their eldest sibling. They were both adorable, especially my brother, who was a joy. We formed a strong bond early on, even though I had to leave when he was just one. Fortunately, I returned when he was three, and our bond deepened. Yet, I had to leave again, missing out on significant parts of his childhood. Back then, long-distance communication was pricey, and keeping in touch was tough without the convenience of video calls. He now lives far away but has made a good life for himself. Thanks to technology, we manage to stay connected. Seeing him is always refreshing, even if he's just stepping back into a room after a short while.

My sister, my constant supporter, played a crucial role in my life. It felt like we were both navigating the challenges of our household together, especially with a stepdad who was mostly difficult (though he's okay now). Life was tough, but our bond remained strong. I've always felt a protective urge towards her. She was outgoing and talkative, capable of engaging with anyone, and always speaking her mind, no matter how wild or inappropriate her thoughts seemed at a young age. Our relationship is stronger than ever today. She remains my biggest supporter, still humorous and straightforward.

Honesty was drilled into us growing up. My dad only had to get physical with me once, and it was because I lied. My sister, on the other hand, lied a lot, and my mom would lose it, telling her that the "devil was her Father" because he is the father of lies. So, lying wasn't something we were encouraged to do, and frankly, I'm terrible at remembering lies anyway, so what's the point? I did have a knack for spinning tales as a teenager, though. I could cook up stories that were just believable enough to fool some people. But that's a whole other story.

Religion? That was a tough sell for me at first. It felt like a bunch of rules and not much fun. Sitting through services at the Kingdom Hall (that's what Jehovah's Witnesses call their church) and enduring all-day assemblies was a snooze-fest, except for lunch. We were supposed to do it to please God, but I wasn't feeling it. My home life was a mess, and the example set by my mom and stepdad, who were Jehovah's Witnesses, didn't inspire me to follow that path. But things change. Eventually, I was drawn to the faith and stuck with it for 19 years as a Jehovah's Witness. That's not where I'm at now, though—I've moved on from the organization. Before I left, religion was a big part of how I figured out how to live and raise my kids. It was like a guidebook, you know? But yeah, that chapter of my life is closed now.

Growing up, I was surrounded by my parents' love, which made life feel amazing. Everything seemed perfect until second grade—my parents split, and the constant moving between them began for me. That's also when the event happened that would change my life forever. One day, I came home to find my father holding a knife to my mother's throat, her eye black and swollen. He threatened, "I can kill you right now if I want to." At six or seven years old, I screamed, trying to enter the room to be with her. Although unsure of what I could have done, my stepmom ushered us into her room, preventing me from helping my mom. Guilt haunted me as I grew up. I used to think about all the ways I could have fought my stepmom to escape the room. It was then that I believe I learned to detach my emotions.

I thought my mom had died because she was suddenly gone. Yet, I don't recall ever treating or viewing my father differently after that incident, which I eventually forgot about for a long time. All I knew was that my mom was gone, and I suspected he had killed her. After I saw what happened between my dad and mom, nobody talked about it. It was like everyone was pretending it didn't happen. I thought my mom was dead, and still, no one said a thing. That was when I started to zone out and escape into my thoughts. It makes me think about whether people are born with borderline personality disorder or if it comes from experiences like that. I've always sought safety in my relationships, especially with men. However, when faced with violence, I could compartmentalize those feelings, separating the person from their actions, just as I did with my father back then.

There was another time I saw something traumatic happen to a loved one. I screamed, and the adults showed up, but I went to school the next day like nothing had happened. I was so young I didn't even have the words to discuss my feelings, but I knew something was wrong. And still, no one said anything. Reflecting on it, I realized a bit later, around fourth and fifth grade, that my mom became more distant and seemed frustrated with me a lot. This tension reached a point where, in sixth grade, I was sent to live with my dad. As time passed, my relationship with my mom grew strained, and it took a while before things started to improve between us.

My dad was always my rock, the constant thing in all the changes. My father always made me feel special. He called me "sunshine". When I got pregnant at 18, everything shifted. That's when he stopped calling me "sunshine". He was a constant source of comfort, always smiling at me and making me feel important. Until he didn't, there were times when he got upset and wouldn't talk to me, icing me out and leaving me feeling terrible without ever really knowing what I had done to upset him. That felt like torture, though it didn't happen all that often. But when it did, it devastated me. I felt like he was all I had in life, the one person who truly loved me or the parent who cared, or at least seemed to. He shipped me off, too, so it wasn't just my mother. If I became too much, no one knew what to do. I missed him after he left San Diego in 4th grade, especially when things started to get hard, particularly after my stepdad came into the picture—though he wasn't my stepdad yet, just my mom's boyfriend.

My childhood memories are mixed. There were the funny moments, like eating a rose or watching my mom make ice cream out of snow, and the bittersweet ones, like saying goodbye to a family friend when I was too young to get what was happening. I had my share of adventures, from sliding down the stairs on pillows to claiming the top bunk in our RV. As time went on, I noticed I could detach from anything. Dissociating became something I could do whenever I wanted, making me feel like whatever was happening wasn't real. I started acting out as a teenager, withdrawing from others, and turning to drinking and smoking weed—anything to escape. Back then, I didn't realize what I was running from or even that I was trying to escape. I wasn't really into relationships, but eventually, I felt I needed to be in one to have a baby. I didn't love the baby's father, barely liked him, but he was protective, which I thought I needed. He could be intense and sometimes rough, especially when I was upset and 'acting crazy,' as he put it. I often blamed myself and dealt with it, like I always did.

Eventually, I married a guy who wasn't right for me (more on that later). Going through that marriage and then a divorce felt like one mistake after another. I never saw a bright future for myself. I thought I'd either die young or end up taking my own life. Having my first son gave me a reason to keep going, even though I always worried I'd leave him too soon. Ironically, he left me early, but that's another story.

When I was almost an adult, at 17, I faced a challenging situation with a man I thought I could trust. We connected over writing and poetry, and he seemed harmless. One day, he asked me to bring my writing to his house. I felt at ease at first because he was a familiar face, but he became someone else within minutes. He pinned me down, and I was terrified I was going to be raped. I fought back as hard as I could, screaming and trying to kick him off, but he was too strong. Eventually, when I started to give up, he stopped and let me go. I told my friend and her mom (who was his friend), but he denied everything, claiming I was just a young girl with a crush, which was false.

This experience and others made me always wary of men, always assessing whether I could defend myself against them. It shaped my belief that if something bad happened while I was alone with a man, it was somehow my fault—a constant and troubling outlook that lasted into my 40s. Whenever something bad happened, whether I was younger or as I got older, I found myself reacting in whatever way I could—sometimes I froze, other times I just gave in, especially when it felt like fighting back was useless. When I was 14, I told a social worker once, and they called the cops, but nothing came of it. It was just another reminder that speaking up didn't change anything.

I was with a friend who had an older boyfriend. He brought a friend with him to visit. He was very tall and very cute. He knew I was 13. He was 19, and I thought it was cool that he was interested in me. We rode around the city and back to my friend's house. I didn't know a thing about boys or how they operated. I didn't know anything really about sex either. It's not like anyone sat down and talked about it, God forbid. So, when he pushed me on the bed, I didn't know what was going on when I felt him try and enter me. I was like, wait, what the hell, and I jumped up. I should have figured out how to leave, but I didn't. I was shocked and didn't know what was happening. He ended up talking to me about different things. I was settled down, thinking the sex part was over, and we were just gonna talk. I was stuck at my friends', so where was I going? His friend was still there, so where was he going? I told him it was okay to kiss me. So, he did a lot outside. Later, we went inside to watch TV, and he did more than kiss me, and I was frozen like, what the hell is happening? I couldn't move. I didn't want to go any further with him. I swear I didn't want to, and I told him that. I told him

I didn't want to more than once, but there was so much pressure. After so much hounding, I eventually gave in and said forget it. I didn't know what else to do. I didn't know coercion was a thing. I didn't know at 13 I wasn't even old enough to give consent to a 19-year-old.

Later, we ended up meeting again at a gathering with friends, and that time was a forced situation. I should have left when I saw him in hindsight, but at that moment, I didn't know about sexual coercion or that he had done anything wrong. I thought it was me. He kept talking to me. We were all drinking. I somehow ended up in the lay-down position with him laughing and talking. I didn't 'realize I was in a bad situation again. This time was worse than the first time cause this time, I kept telling him to stop, and he wouldn't. This time, my friend and his friend were there, and they said nothing. Then he raped me. Maybe they didn't hear me, I'm not sure. I had a social worker I was seeing at school, and I told her about this inadvertently. She told me it was rape and called the school police officer. There wasn't anything they could do. And honestly, I didn't want to do anything anyhow. I just wanted to forget the situation, which had drawn too much attention.

In my younger years, my living situation was unique. Living with my mom, dad, and stepmom felt normal. Reflecting on the unique living arrangement with my parents and stepmother, I don't believe it had a noticeable impact during my childhood, simply because I didn't know any different. However, this setup shaped my views on relationships and family structures as I matured. I grew to see having multiple partners as not particularly concerning, though not the life I chose for myself. My father's actions likely influenced this perspective; my mom and stepmom weren't the only ones he was involved with, although delving into those stories wasn't my place. My upbringing sparked a curiosity about polygamy. It's a lifestyle that fascinates me, and I find myself drawn to various shows about polygamous relationships, both religious-based and those like Sister Wives.

Dealing with hardships? Well, I learned to bottle up feelings pretty early on. I often turned to food for emotional support. Unfortunately, that led me to morbid obesity. I've been overweight my entire life, but now, at 50, the consequences have caught up with me in the form of medical issues I'm struggling to manage. Being significantly larger than my peers was always on my mind. In my youth, it didn't hinder me physically, except for limitations like being unable to jump fences or run for long periods. Interestingly, it didn't drastically affect my social life either; boys were still interested in me as I got older, and I only faced minimal teasing. My weight went largely unaddressed by those around me, including my family, as if it were a non-issue.

There was a point when my mom and I tried Nutrisystem together, and I managed to lose some weight, though it was challenging. I wasn't prone to binge eating, but I had a weakness for sweets and carbs. My dad was a frequent cook, and there was always an abundance of food at his house, contributing to my weight gain, especially during my time in Dover. I was more active in California, but the abundance of food was a constant, and my difficult relationship with my stepdad and my mom's apparent dislike made food a source of comfort. Even today, whether I'm stressed or happy, I turn to food, but I'm finally starting to gain control over it.

I came to find comfort in solitude, learning the hard way that some feelings are better kept to oneself. When times got tough, I often felt alone. Sure, in my younger years, school and friends provided some escape. And yes, my brother and sister were unknowing pillars of support, their mere presence a beacon of hope and laughter in an otherwise confusing world.

At age 13, I was sent back to San Diego just when I had adjusted to living in Dover for two years, and honestly, I wasn't thrilled about it. However, I eventually settled in and was happy to reunite with my siblings, but that happiness was short-lived. The presence of my stepdad and stepsiblings made life difficult. My mom seemed to care that I was alive, but that's about it, and I was deeply unhappy. To escape, I spent a lot of time with my friends, smoking weed and drinking. My stepdad didn't like me; he seemed constantly annoyed by even the smallest things, like leaving suds in the sink after washing dishes—a stark contrast to the more laid-back atmosphere I grew used to with my dad in Dover.

There was a significant fight eventually, leading to my stepdad moving out, which briefly made life seem better. I remember expressing my happiness to my mom in the car, telling her how glad I was. It was just us again, only for her to respond, "Do you think I want to be alone for the rest of my life because of you?" That moment marked the last time I confided in her for years. To this day, I don't feel completely emotionally safe with her, though things have improved slightly in recent years. Despite a generally good relationship now, we don't share a bond where deep feelings are exchanged. Our connection simply doesn't extend to that level. Emotional connections, in general, are something I don't experience except with my sister and a person who has recently come into my life.

Eventually, we all ended up back together, my stepfamily, mom, and biological siblings, which was far from ideal. While there were moments of fun with some of my stepsiblings, any sense of joy or acceptance was absent when it came to my stepdad. He seemed to despise me, fueling a dark wish within me against him. Amidst this chaos, I felt a strong urge to protect my sister, though I wasn't exactly sure what from—perhaps just the constant turmoil at home, where criticism was the norm and praise was non-existent, unlike the warm welcomes at my dad's house.

I never felt accepted at home; it was as if I didn't belong there. Being away felt better, and sometimes, my friends' parents provided the comfort that my mother couldn't. As mentioned, I learned not to turn to her for emotional support; it seemed beyond her capacity. Her complaints or criticisms quickly shut down any attempts. At times, I wished for her undivided attention, for my stepdad and his children to just disappear. My mom and stepdad didn't have a great relationship and hardly set a positive example of family life. I'm sure I was the topic of many of their arguments.

I didn't feel stable at any point. It was like, at any moment, I could be told it was time to pack up and leave again. My house wasn't a home in the true sense, where you're accepted no matter what. It was more like waiting around until someone decided they were sick enough of me to say, "Okay, time to go." When I was around 15 or 16 and left my mom's house to live with my aunt (this was my 4th or 5th transfer), I soon wanted to return home. But the truth hit me hard when I realized 'home' didn't exist for me. I was naive to think it did. When I contacted my mom about coming back, her response was a gut punch: "We're happier without you." So, I stayed with my aunt for however many months until my dad decided to step in and send for me. Being at my aunt's was cool, hanging out with my cousins and all, but trying to fit in at school was a nightmare. I skipped a lot, going to school and then bailing to return to my aunt's house. Eventually, she caught on to what I was doing. Getting busted for skipping school might have pushed me back to living with my dad.

I didn't feel like I belonged anywhere, even if my aunt's house was much more peaceful, loving, and secure than living with my mom. My aunt was kind, especially when I told her about what my mom had said. She tried to empathize, saying she kind of felt the same about one of her kids once, but it didn't come off as harsh when she said it. Moving back to Dover was another big change. The friends I had before were still here, but things weren't the same. We weren't friends anymore. I just dropped off the radar one day and never came back. Time moved on, and we barely talked except for some awkward exchanges. I felt out of place again. Living in San Diego, I'd gone through so much that these folks back in Dover, living their slow-paced lives, couldn't even begin to understand. Dover was slow. San Diego was anything but.

While in San Diego, I often felt out of place at home, as if I were invisible to those around me—except for my sister and brother, who were my lifesavers. This lack of acceptance led me to seek belonging in places and with people who might not have had my best interests at heart. I found myself gravitating towards those involved in drugs and gangs, although my drug use was limited to weed. But my social circle wasn't just confined to them; I was open to everyone, from nerds to skaters. I didn't stick to one specific group; I was a part of a diverse mix, always searching for a place where I truly belonged.

When I think back, I can't trace how my friendships started; they happened. I'm not a people person, but somehow, people like me. Even when I'm hoping they'd leave me alone, they stick around, and just like that, a friendship forms. Between 13 and 15, these friends were everything to me because my home life was pretty miserable. Watching their families, where love was openly shown, made a big difference. They also extended that warmth and support to me, which was something special.

My best friend lived with her mom and grandma. Her grandma was the sweetest lady, and their home always welcomed me. Another friend of mine lived with her mom, who was battling stomach cancer. It was heartbreaking to see, yet their home was filled with love and great advice. I remember how their house was always warm, not just temperature-wise but in the feeling it gave off. One time, I asked why my house felt like a freezer compared to theirs, and she said it was because theirs was filled with love. I believed it. Being in their homes made me wish to live there instead of mine.

Having these friends and being welcomed into their families gave me the social interactions and care that were missing in my home. Sometimes, I even got the discipline that was absent at my house. Discipline at my house was usually just someone yelling or criticizing for no good reason. My curfew was supposedly 10 pm, but honestly, who cared? I didn't. I'd much rather crash at a friend's house or sleep outside than go home.

Talking about discipline, once my mom tried to ground me for the weekend. I was with her at the store and asked if she was serious. Part of me was impressed that she was attempting discipline. But then she backtracked, asking if I thought she wanted me around all weekend. So off I went. There were times I'd ground myself if I felt I was getting too wild, usually after drinking or finding myself in risky situations. And while my mom probably imagined the worst, like me sleeping around, it was never about that. It was more about drinking, roaming downtown San Diego, and hanging out in not-so-great places with not-so-great people.

When I was 13, my mother attacked me with a broom handle. I had been out all night. I came home at the standard be home before noon the next day time slot, and there she was pissed off. We had an obvious miscommunication. I didn't care too much because, on this day, I didn't even want to come home. The night before was the first time I'd ever had a sexual encounter, and I didn't want to. I didn't realize until recently that what happened to me was sexual assault. I didn't know then. Who was I going to talk to? The woman who met me at the door with a broom handle. I didn't care about the broomstick; I felt numb and distraught while walking there. I figured I'd better scream and act like this woman was hurting me so she could feel better or proud of herself or whatever it was she was thinking she was accomplishing. Inside, I was dead, and I hated that house more and more every day. The bruises I was left with on my thighs meant nothing to cause; the scars and pain in my head would always outweigh them.

Trauma has been a significant part of my life for quite some time. Reflecting on my most traumatizing experiences, one that stands out vividly is being in an emotionally abusive marriage. In 2000, I thought I loved someone enough to marry them, but I didn't foresee the disaster it would become. I was naive about addiction and the lengths to which an addict would go to satisfy their cravings. Moreover, my intense fear of abandonment led me to a 20-year lesson in the extremes of addictive behavior. I became more vigilant while being with my husband, which became my norm—always on edge, always anticipating the next crisis. I found myself covering for him constantly; if he binged all night and couldn't work the next day, I would make excuses to keep our son and his employer in the dark.

Aron struggled with substance abuse. During our first marriage, someone came to our door demanding money because Aron had bought drugs from him while he was supposed to be taking out the trash. I was nervous dealing with this person, but I convinced him never to return to our door. Unfortunately, this was not an isolated incident. Aron frequently interacted with dealers and would often sell his phone. I'd call him only to have a stranger answer, and I would then have to meet these people to retrieve the phone.

This constant fear of who might be knocking on my door weighed heavily on me. When Aron was under the influence of alcohol, his speech was slurred, and he acted erratically. He was out of it most of the time. During his drug binges, he would disappear, so I rarely saw him under the influence of drugs. I was always on high alert, constantly wondering what would happen next. I could never relax. Even during the rare times when he went months clean and sober, just as I thought it was all over and allowed myself to breathe, he would relapse. I felt I had to remain vigilant, even during the semi-good times.

Aron became aggressive at times. He was very unpredictable. I remember early in our marriage, we were at a nightclub, and he didn't like the attention I was getting. He hit me right in the face. I was in shock. This time, however, I had friends who would have destroyed him if they knew what he had done. I didn't tell them. We just left, and I did a lot of screaming at him that came to nothing.

Once, after he struck me, he began to destroy our apartment in what seemed like an attempt to deflect from his actions toward me. In desperation, I unscrewed a leg from a kitchen chair and threatened him with it, demanding he stop. The next morning, I had to concoct a story for my eight-year-old son, making it seem like the chaos had been an accident. I often found myself feeling overwhelmed trying to raise two children in the home with a person who could not control himself. Between covering for him, protecting my belongings, protecting my kids, and protecting him, I was emotionally depleted. I went to therapy a few times during our marriage, but it was just venting sessions about what Aron was doing, with no real tips on how to separate myself mentally or help myself. I felt lost in my mind, stuck with a man I couldn't stand. The most common emotions I felt were despair and frustration. My outlook on life was bleak. I lived for my children and thought I was living for God. God was one of the main reasons I kept fighting to stay with this man, thinking I was doing the right thing. But I was miserable, sad, and alone.

I saw myself as a failure and a confused person. I didn't see someone awesome in the mirror; I felt bleak. My self-esteem and self-worth were in the trash. I longed for a real marriage filled with love, family, joy, and stability, but I didn't have it. We rarely spoke to each other, and little love was shown daily. I felt ugly inside and out, bonded to Aron in a way that felt inescapable. Despite the misery and his terrible behavior, there were times when he seemed to be the only person who understood me.

I hoped that if he could just overcome his issues with drugs and alcohol, we could have a good marriage. The idea of him leaving made my chest hurt; I was distraught. I didn't know about codependency or trauma bonding then. I just knew I didn't want to be left alone again. I didn't want to lose the person I thought helped put my mind at ease, even though he caused more havoc than happiness. I felt like a failure as a mother. I wanted our son to have a father because they got along so well during his younger days. They were so much alike and had lots of fun together. I tried to shield our son from the reality of Aron's alcohol binges, but sometimes, it was impossible to hide when Aron would disappear for days or steal from the house.

There were so many moments during my marriage when I felt deeply ashamed or embarrassed about something I did or was forced to do. One of the most vivid memories was when my young son was very sick and hospitalized. Aron visited the first day but then disappeared, leaving me alone at the hospital with our son. He never returned or called. After four days, when our son was released, Aron decided to come home. I told him he could stay on the couch because I didn't have the energy to deal with him. Financially dependent on him, he had more control than I wanted. My older son came home, saw Aron there, packed his belongings, and left. He couldn't take it anymore and threatened to call child protection if I didn't stop letting Aron come around. I was embarrassed and wished I could tell Aron to leave and never return, but I didn't know how to survive financially. I am very ashamed I got myself into that position and regret not reaching the final moment he had to go. I wish I could apologize to my older son for letting that happen.

In 2002, Aron went on a drug binge and robbed a convenience store. It was on the news and radio, and people I knew heard about it. I was so embarrassed I could have died. Years later, he stole from a disabled gentleman he worked with. That was also on the news, and his picture was posted online. These incidents were deeply humiliating. I found myself making excuses for Aron's behavior to others all the time. I either avoided talking about it or ended up in conversations about his abusive childhood or generational addiction. My Jehovah's Witness friends had a soft spot for him, even when he was ousted from the congregation. They always urged me to support him because of what he had been through. Aron was charming and friendly, and everyone liked him. It was painful to see this because I knew who he was. I was slowly dying inside while the world thought he was wonderful, focusing on his good qualities that weren't always present at home. Even when he wasn't bingeing, we weren't necessarily happy, at least not on my end.

Sometimes, Aron made me do things I was uncomfortable with or didn't want to do. He would ask me to lie for him, like telling his bosses he was sick when he wasn't or that I was sick and needed him to take care of me. I also had to pick up his checks when he disappeared from jobs and was finally fired. While he didn't force me, he could convince me of almost anything. I felt conflicted and reluctant but didn't see any alternatives. My mind was always confused, and I knew nothing about boundaries or owning my truth. Aron took advantage of this. Sometimes, I did what he wanted to get some peace, even temporarily. Looking back, I feel angry at myself. I wonder how I put up with such foolishness and lived in such a distorted reality. I don't want to say I was brainwashed being a Jehovah's Witness, but I believed I had to sacrifice myself to please God. It was incredibly hard.

As time went on, explaining things to my son became increasingly difficult. Aron stole money, game systems, and pills from our house. He even sold our car for drugs on multiple occasions. The first time he sold the car for drugs, I was blindsided; I didn't even know such things happened. He traded it to a drug dealer, I happened to know. When I tracked down the dealer, I discovered he was in jail. Visiting him there, I finally learned the whereabouts of my car. Retrieving it involved venturing into a rough neighborhood, but I got my car back. That day was a harsh lesson in the realities of addiction.

As time passed, my vigilance increased to the point where I began sleeping with the car keys under my pillow. If they were visible, I risked waking up to find the car gone. Even hiding them under the mattress didn't ease my anxiety; I feared he might find them whenever I left the room, even just to use the bathroom. My life became a series of rapid showers, always rushing, fearful of what might happen in my absence. Despite all this, I stayed with him for years.

Late in our marriage, there was another incident where he pushed my head so hard that I ended up with a concussion. He was upset, and I was arguing back when he forcefully pushed my forehead. It wasn't a strike, but the impact made my head swing backward. He left so quickly afterward that I had no chance to respond. I compartmentalized that experience and soon let it go. Years passed without further violence, but I never stopped being on guard, always waiting for the other shoe to drop. That night, it did, and I was completely unprepared—a lapse in judgment I regret. It's embarrassing to acknowledge all the times I covered for him, tolerated the intolerable, or simply checked out. I keep asking myself, why didn't I leave permanently? Looking back, I see that my deep-seated fear of abandonment trapped me in this harmful situation for most of my adult life.

As time went on with Aron, I became increasingly withdrawn from everyone else. Most of my time was either hiding Aron's misdeeds or monitoring him so closely that I had no time for anything else. I was numb, just getting through life without truly experiencing it. Despite this, for some reason, I couldn't bear the thought of him leaving. The fear of being alone seemed worse than enduring the constant turmoil. I guess I was resigned to living in isolation, caught in a relentless cycle of panic, anxiety, numbness, and dissociation.

Sometimes, I lost track of time; days blurred together, and I couldn't remember when things happened. There was so much gaslighting—although I didn't know the term then—and it left me confused, a state Aron exploited to his advantage. I often couldn't tell if I was coming or going, which made it easier for him to manipulate situations because I might not remember incidents clearly. If I was upset about something he had done, he could nearly convince me of anything, frequently blaming my confusion on borderline personality disorder (BPD). I didn't have the energy to fight back. It was just like the trauma responses I had years before freeze, go numb, dissociate, and keep moving.

Having BPD, my sense of self-identity was already fragile. Being bonded with Aron and identifying as his wife became a significant part of my identity. I didn't know what else was out there. Life in my head wasn't always pleasant. Most of the time, I thought I was losing my mind, and Aron was the only person who truly understood how I felt. He knew how often I mentally checked out, sometimes for days. When I returned to the present, I was always confused. How could I explain that to anyone when I barely understood it myself? I was on autopilot—being a mother, a halfway decent mother if I could manage it. My identity was solely that of a wife and mother.

I had to suppress many aspects of my personality and interests because of Aron's influence. Laughing too much would earn me a disdainful stare, singing loudly and off-key was discouraged, and expressing general happiness was often met with, "What are you so happy for?" His reactions would burst my bubble, causing me to retreat into my mind. Aron's behavior and the compromises I made drastically changed my perception of myself and my capabilities. I felt I had to lessen myself to get along in the marriage. If I was happy, it was a problem. If I had friends, he was jealous. He was especially jealous of my close relationship with my family, particularly my sister because he didn't have close family ties. I never reached my full potential because I was always dampening my personality. Even at work, I couldn't share my triumphs or positive experiences. He was jealous of how long I had been at my job and how much people liked me despite being liked wherever he went. However, I knew his charm was just a front, hiding a shallow and hollow interior.

The fear of abandonment seemed to rule my existence. I couldn't handle the emotional toll of someone leaving or detaching from me. If I had known the tools I learned in Dialectical Behavior Therapy back then, I might have conquered the extreme anxiety I felt when I needed to separate from Aron. Those emotions were overwhelming, and I had no skills to manage them. I knew I had BPD for years, but I didn't understand how much-heightened emotions played a part in it or how to manage them.

I believe I was in a true trauma bond with Aron. Despite the emotional trauma and hardships I endured because of him, he was also the person I turned to when I was falling apart. He knew how crazy I could get. He knew that self-harm was always at the front of my mind, and he knew I was terrified of losing people whenever I made a "mistake." He knew everything, and even though his actions caused most of my turmoil, I couldn't separate myself from him. I didn't understand why at the time.

My parents' inconsistent presence in my life significantly influenced my reluctance to leave my husband. I felt like my parents would ship me off at the drop of a hat. If I made a mistake or fell out of line, I was sent somewhere else, becoming someone else's problem. My dad either sent me to my mom or kicked me out of the house to fend for myself. When something I did set him off, he would shut me out completely. I didn't belong anywhere, especially not at my parents' homes. After I turned 10, I was a guest in their houses, not a household member.

Aron was the first thing that was truly mine. Despite all the chaos, he seemed to accept me. When we met, I had a lot to handle. Though he had his addiction, which I didn't fully understand, his acceptance became so addicting to me. I thought, "This is mine. This is a place to belong." Even though that feeling was short-lived, I always wanted it back and didn't lose sight of the possibility it could return, so I stayed.

I realize now how I misled myself into thinking I was the cause of my trauma by staying in a toxic relationship. I should never have stayed; the responsibility for enduring so much pain lies with me. I would have been far better off single during those 20 years. Believing that things would change after he became a Jehovah's Witness was incredibly naive—one of the most misguided beliefs I've ever held.

Reflecting on my childhood, I realize that the lack of a stable, supportive environment shaped my understanding of a healthy relationship. I saw my parents' relationships as normal, even though they were far from it. Living with my mom, dad, and stepmom under the same roof seemed normal until I later realized it wasn't. My mom and stepdad didn't get along, and she stayed despite not being happy. My dad treated my stepmom like she didn't exist most of the time and would snap at her occasionally. I never saw joy or true happiness in their marriages. When I became a Jehovah's Witness, I learned about the potential of relationships, and I hoped that if Aron could stay off drugs and alcohol, we could have that kind of relationship. But it never happened, not even during his dry spells.

To cope with the trauma of my childhood, I developed dissociation and emotional detachment, which affected my ability to recognize and respond to the abuse in my marriage. I knew it was horrible, but I wasn't sure it was abusive. Aron's violent outbursts were long ago, so I wasn't constantly battered, and I wasn't meek or silent. I thought I was just dealing with marriage as I was supposed to, enduring long-suffering as Jehovah's Witnesses are taught. In that process, I became a shell of a person, constantly dissociating.

During my marriage, I relied on coping mechanisms from my childhood, like writing. When I could, I'd write about the things I couldn't express out loud, but that stopped because Aron would read everything. I had no real privacy. Singing was another outlet, and even though I'm not a good singer, it helped release my emotions. Sometimes, I just mentally checked out. I would retreat into my brain, sometimes knowingly and without realizing it, until I returned to the present.

There were many instances where I emotionally shut down or dissociated in response to Aron's actions. We went to counseling a few times together, but I shut down because Aron was such a good talker that he convinced the therapist the problem was me. It felt pointless to go. He could charm anyone in counseling, around friends, at our congregation, with my family, or his family. I stayed silent and waited for the show to be over. He was the mouthpiece, and I was shut down. At times, I found comfort in his ability to take over, not realizing he was the reason I was so shut down.

The critical and unsupportive environment of my childhood severely affected my self-esteem and sense of self-worth, making me more vulnerable to accepting abusive behavior in my marriage. Growing up, I always felt something was wrong, as if I was broken. I believed that if I belonged somewhere, I would feel whole. Joining the Jehovah's Witnesses gave me a sense of belonging, and the negative messages of doubt and self-criticism initially faded.

My efforts to gain approval and avoid criticism as a child translated into my behavior and choices in my marriage. I often treated Aron disdainfully, much like my mom treated my stepdad. His actions made me sick, and it was hard not to show it. When Aron had drug or alcohol issues and the elders (the heads of the congregation in the Jehovah Witness religion) met with us, I was often lectured for my attitude. My attitude was a response to Aron's actions, but that didn't matter. He made me sick, and it was hard for me not to act like it.

Looking back, I can identify patterns and cycles from my childhood that repeated in my marriage. Feeling powerless or voiceless as a child resurfaced in my marital relationship. I felt powerless when I relied on Aron financially and didn't know what to do, even when I felt emotionally ready to leave him. It took a while, but I eventually became completely sick of him. However, financial dependency kept us tied together. Talking to him was like talking to a rock, so it became pointless.

My early experiences of feeling unwanted or not belonging shaped my interactions and decisions in my marriage. When Aron came along, I felt like I finally belonged somewhere. We shared a talent for writing poems and stories and had issues with our parents. He loved me for who I was, not for any other reason. We connected through our use of alcohol as a numbing agent. I drank a lot when we met, but I couldn't stop, which I did shortly after we met. He never did. Despite not loving him anymore, I thought I belonged with him and didn't want to abandon him.

As I think about the years I spent with Aron, there was a lot I didn't understand. I did get an eight-year break when he was in jail, but we were still connected in some ways. I sometimes feel stupid, but those feelings lessen as I think about how my life and mind were affected by having BPD and not having a place where I felt I belonged growing up. Understanding the root of many of my behaviors and decisions does help. I don't blame the past, but I can see how my fear of abandonment had a grip on me. It's embarrassing to even write about these things, the few out of many, that I experienced with my ex-husband. But today, I know I'd never let those things happen again. Today, I know I'm stronger, I have a voice, and I would use it. I've learned that love doesn't mean suffering, contrary to what my old religion taught me. That was part of why I stayed in such a bad situation for so long, thinking I was doing the right thing.

By connecting my past experiences with my behavior in my marriage, I've gained valuable insights about myself. I've realized that I'm not as horrible as I once thought. I'm learning to feel less and less ashamed of my actions. I now understand BPD better, particularly the lack of self-identity and the attachment issues that come with it. I see that these issues stemmed from my childhood experiences, over which I had no control. It was my parents' job to parent me, not my job to figure out life on my own. While I don't blame them entirely for my mistakes, I recognize how my upbringing shaped my personality and my personality disorder. I had no control over any of that.

I am actively working to break the patterns and cycles from my childhood that contributed to my tolerance of an abusive marriage. Dialectical behavior therapy (DBT) has been life-changing. Through DBT, I've worked on healing my inner child and learned not to abandon myself. I now understand what self-abandonment is and refuse to let it happen again. I see my value simply for existing, independent of my past. This newfound understanding and self-worth are helping me move forward in a healthier, more positive direction.

I have learned to set and maintain boundaries and understand values important to me, not necessarily preached from a podium. I can uphold these values and surround myself with people who respect them. It's an ongoing process that requires constant work. I now know how to maintain my emotional balance and regain stability when they become unmanageable. Therapy, both individual and group, has been the most effective support for me. Since my first introduction to DBT in 2001, I have never stopped practicing those skills. I am confident that I will never again be the person who accepts anything just to avoid dealing with it. I will not dissociate and miss out on my own life again.

I have begun to address and heal from the shame and embarrassment I felt during my marriage by owning my actions. I acknowledge that I did those things but won't do them again. I speak kindly to myself and remind myself that I am different now. I have openly talked about how bad things got with Aron and admitted my foolishness despite feeling ashamed. Writing this chapter means anyone who reads it will know some of what I have done, though it's impossible to capture it all.

To reclaim my identity and rebuild my self-esteem since leaving the marriage, I have focused on learning about myself. I've learned to be comfortable in my head and skin. Positive self-talk and associating with uplifting people have been crucial. I left the religious organization that filled me with constant guilt and a sense of never being good enough. However, I left with gratitude and no ill will. I am discovering who I am and doing what I enjoy. I no longer seek external validation or a place to belong because I belong wherever I am, comfortable with myself—which is a gift.

LETTER TO SELF

Dear Younger Me,

I know you feel lost and alone like no one cares, and you can barely manage in a world you don't belong in. Your life will be full of challenges that may get worse before they get better. But I assure you, better days will come. You are stronger than your struggles. You are not who your brain tries to convince you that you are. You deserve all the good things life has to offer, and there is a lot that life has to offer. You are not alone because I am with you now. I will make sure you are safe and protected and learn all the tools you need to get through life without feeling alone, abandoned, or stupid for the actions you took when you didn't know what your other choices were.

Forgive yourself for situations that occurred when you didn't know how to get through them—situations that were not your fault when you weren't protected by the people who should have protected you or been there for you. You are going to be fine. You got this. Your past does not determine your future. The past has shaped you into the resilient, wonderful person you are. Your story will show others that challenges are stepping stones through struggles and don't have to make you fall.

Every time you were discarded, faced adversity, or felt like life was not worth living, you persevered. When you felt stuck, you eventually managed to find a way out. There is nothing you have faced that you haven't gotten through. Every day, you continue to show your resilience. Celebrate each step you make in your healing journey. You are not defined by what has happened to you. You can have a life full of love, laughter, and gratitude. You will have a partner to support you through that healing journey who will help you see the value in yourself. That's your sister Alisa, always your cheerleader. You will inspire and encourage her, which will make your heart joyful.

You are not defined by how you have been treated. You can make mistakes and still be worthy of support, kindness, and acceptance. You will eventually do more than just get through things; you will thrive. You will know how to manage. You will have a life worth living, and you deserve it.

With love and compassion,
~ Michelle

CHAPTER SEVEN

Scorched But Not Burned

Nicole Pierce

Imagine the loneliness of feeling misunderstood, the confusion of mixed messages from those who are supposed to guide and nurture. Trust is a foreign concept; love is conditional, fleeting, and often intertwined with hurt. The child learns to mask their true feelings and hide behind a mask while their inner world is turned upside down. This is the backdrop, the setting of a life shaped by the storms of childhood, a life still searching for the calm after the storm.

My life began on November 28th, 1988, in Newark, Delaware. Later, I moved to Brooklyn, New York, where I embarked on a journey of complex familial ties and self-discovery. Growing up with six siblings, my family dynamics were divided between my mother's and father's sides, setting the stage for a childhood filled with contrasting relationships. Out of the four siblings on my mother's side, I only grew up with two: my oldest sister and my youngest sister. My older brother was in and out of jail, so our relationship was very inconsistent, especially with visiting him in prison.

I didn't meet my brothers on my dad's side until later in life. I met my brother "CJ" when I was 11, when my dad sent for us to come to California. I didn't meet my youngest brother "Kevin" until I was an adult in my twenties. I felt a stronger sense of belonging on my mom's side. I didn't see my brothers on my dad's side often enough to build a relationship with them. However, as they got older, the relationship-building seemed forced.

I shared a complicated bond with my mom, one filled with both love and resentment. Growing up, her treatment was often harsh and marked by verbal abuse that left lasting scars. I often felt attacked when she chastised me or got angry. Compliments from her were rare, and her harsh words hurt my self-esteem. Her constant criticism was like a hammer, chipping away at my sense of self-worth. I remember feeling crushed when she dismissed my efforts or achievements with a few cutting words. Her voice became the loudest in my head, reinforcing my insecurities and causing me to doubt my abilities.

Already struggling with low self-esteem, any criticism felt enormous to me, making me feel even more inadequate. Even when I got good grades, it never seemed enough to earn her approval. This sense of not measuring up followed me into adulthood, affecting my personal and professional growth. Her disapproval cast a long shadow over my life, making it hard to shake off the feeling that I was never good enough. It was as if her negative words had taken root deep inside me, blossoming into a persistent belief that I was fundamentally flawed.

Starting my own business was a big deal, and when she offered her help, it felt like she was finally supporting me. However, the wounds from the past made it difficult to fully trust her intentions. Over time, we've gotten closer, and I've become better at setting boundaries with her. At first, it felt like I had to prove myself to earn her support. When we'd argue, she'd sometimes throw her financial help in my face, which hurt, reopening old wounds and reminding me of the power imbalance that had always been there. But things have started to change between us. The day she told me she was proud of me hit home. It felt like a huge win, showing me how far we've come in understanding and respecting each other.

My dad's presence in my life was pretty inconsistent. He left when I was about five and returned during my teenage years, but he never really stuck around. This shaped how I view trust and reliability in relationships. I learned not to trust easily because whenever my dad reappeared, it always felt like he had ulterior motives. It seemed like he only showed up when he wanted something, and once he got it, he'd disappear again. This pattern made it hard for me to trust anyone deeply. As a result, in my relationships with men, I never fully committed or became anyone's girlfriend.

My earliest childhood memories are vividly set in Brooklyn, where outdoor play and community gatherings painted a picture of a vibrant but challenging youth. I spent a lot of time with my siblings and cousins under the watchful eyes of the neighborhood. However, there was always a subtle competition, especially with my aunt Tina, who made sure her daughter stood out among us.

Regarding my extended family, I've consciously decided to distance myself from them. Although there were some great experiences with them, the more painful, embarrassing, and humiliating moments stand out the most. It's not that I don't love them, but being around them often serves as a constant reminder of those difficult times. Growing up, the teasing from cousins and the perceived favoritism within the family often made me feel inadequate and less valued. My Aunt Tina's constant efforts to make her daughter shine the brightest among us only intensified these feelings. This environment of subtle competition and comparison left a lasting impact on my self-esteem and how I viewed myself about others.

These negative experiences overshadowed the good times, making being around my extended family hard without feeling those old wounds resurface. The constant reminders of my struggles with self-worth and the emotional pain I endured made it difficult to maintain close relationships with them. Distancing myself was a way to protect my emotional well-being, allowing me the space to heal and grow without the constant reminder of those painful memories.

After leaving New York, I felt a sense of relief, as if I could leave behind the weight of those painful memories. While I don't hold any hard feelings towards my family, I've chosen not to engage with them for my emotional well-being. Prioritizing my mental health has meant focusing on building relationships outside of the extended family circle, where I can find support and positivity without the baggage of past hurts.

School achievements gave me a brief sense of validation, but my mom's unpredictable reactions often left me feeling inadequate. Even when I received recognition at school, my mom's backhanded compliments took away from those moments. These things impacted how I chased achievements later in life. Despite getting awards, I felt like they didn't mean much because my mom never fully celebrated or acknowledged them.

This carried into my adult life, where I often downplayed my accomplishments, including starting my own business. Even though I've been successfully running my business for three years, I find myself not talking about it as much as I should, almost like it's not a big deal. This tendency to minimize my achievements comes from my lack of validation and recognition growing up.

Trying to escape the emotional chaos was tough because of practical fears, which summed up my early struggles. Despite these challenges, my relationship with my grandmother and some family members gave me some comfort and support. However, the complicated family dynamics were made worse by my dad's absence and the distant relationships with his side of the family, including my younger brothers.

My older sister became my closest ally, and our shared experiences created a strong bond that helped us get through our tough childhood. Moments like seeing my grandmother in a physical altercation were significant events that made my childhood anything but ordinary. Our coping mechanisms varied during difficult times, from escapism to the creative outlets my sister and I found during moments of punishment. We crafted alternate realities to distract ourselves from the hardships we faced. However, my coping mechanism of creating alternative realities hasn't evolved much over time. Instead, I've noticed a tendency to avoid confronting problems altogether or react with anger when faced with challenges.

For example, in the early stages of my marriage, arguments with my husband would sometimes prompt me to pack my bags and leave, convinced that as an adult, I could simply avoid certain issues. This pattern reflects a defense mechanism where I either defend "little Nikki" by engaging in conflict or withdraw to avoid uncomfortable situations. While this coping mechanism may have provided temporary relief, it hasn't evolved into a healthier approach to handling challenges.

The main source of support during my rough childhood was my oldest sister. I never felt alone in dealing with my trauma because she was always there for me. It's like she has an innate understanding of who I am—I don't have to explain much, and she just gets it. She's one of the few people who truly knows the real me, understanding my emotions and actions better than anyone else. We share a deep connection that goes beyond words, allowing us to relate on a level that others can't comprehend. Even now, as an adult, she remains my go-to person whenever I face problems or need support.

Growing up, my family taught me the importance of sticking together and being careful about who we let into our lives. These values really shaped how I see trust and loyalty today.

My family believed that friends were just associates. This belief instilled in me about having no friends, only associates, has greatly influenced my approach to friendships and social interactions in adulthood. I don't have many friends; I tend to keep a small circle unless it's related to my business. I'm naturally a private person and try not to let people get too close to me. When someone gets close and does something I don't like, I don't hesitate cutting them off. I prefer small social gatherings and often feel uncomfortable and awkward at larger events. I'm not much of a phone person either; I'd rather communicate via text, except when it's with my mom or sisters. My friend circle remains small due to these tendencies shaped by my upbringing.

Throughout my life, I've always struggled to be my true self because I was afraid of being judged or misunderstood. The real "Nikki" often felt like too much for others, so I put on a mask to fit in, even though it wasn't really me. My social life had its normal moments with sleepovers and parties, but there was always an underlying sense of awkwardness. I struggled to be myself while trying to meet everyone else's expectations.

Moving from New York to Delaware brought its own set of challenges. We even stayed in a hotel for a while, which really highlighted the instability and constant changes I experienced growing up. Living in a hotel and constantly moving around really messed with our family dynamics and my sense of security.

Moving from place to place became normal, and I never felt stable. This way of living left a mark on me. Now, I find it hard to stay in one place for too long. Even though I've been living in Dover since 2016, I always feel restless and want change. These experiences made me uncomfortable with stability, and I always crave something new.

As I reflect on my struggle to be true to myself, fear of judgment has always been a heavy weight, impacting my personal relationships and career choices. When it comes to relationships, I've never been one to have a wide circle of close friends. And when it comes to my career, self-doubt often creeps in, making me question every decision I make. I remember vividly a moment from my high school graduation when I shared my dream of attending fashion school with my mom. But instead of encouragement, she shot it down, saying I wouldn't make any money in that field. So, I let go of my dreams of applying to schools like FIT or FIDM. Moments like these stick with me, making me hesitant to fully embrace my love for fashion. I second-guess my outfit choices and sometimes even holding back from wearing makeup. This fear of being judged has seeped into every aspect of my life, shaping my choices and holding me back from pursuing my passions with full force.

Creativity has been my go-to for getting through the rough patches, like dealing with my insecurities about my looks, especially my forehead. But going natural with my hair was a game-changer. Thinking about the big chop and showing off my forehead was scary, but I did it, and it felt amazing. Sure, I hit a bump when I tried wigs and faced some nasty comments, but it only made me more confident in my natural self. It's funny how that worked out, making me proud of sticking to who I am, even when it wasn't the popular choice.

Dealing with my family, especially the tough parts, has really taught me a lot about myself. I've got this resilience and a strong work ethic, and I've learned how to stand on my own two feet. I've faced a lot of "no's" and "you can't do that," but here I am, using that as fuel. My mom might not have been perfect in teaching me about independence, but I got the message – work hard, rely on yourself, and take care of your own stuff. I learned all the essentials young – cooking, cleaning, managing money – the basics a lot of folks my age seem to miss.

I realize now that my mom had her own struggles with processing pain, and it often spilled over into her parenting. She faced many challenges, and unfortunately, her way of coping involved taking out her frustrations on those around her, including me. Understanding this doesn't erase the impact of her words, but it helps me see her as a complex person rather than just the source of my pain.

There have been these sweet spots, though, where I felt seen for my efforts, and it meant the world. Like landing my first gig out of esthetics school and getting that glowing review from a client – it validated everything I was working toward. It reminded me why I pushed through school and refused to quit, even when college didn't pan out.

What I'm most proud of, hands down is not giving up on my esthetics career. Those first two years were brutal, juggling jobs and barely making ends meet. But sticking with it, even after getting laid off during COVID, led me to a great opportunity that's allowed me to work for myself and build something I'm truly proud of. It's a reminder of my own strength and determination.

Stability's always been a bit foreign to me, given all the moving around I did. But settling down with my husband and our kids has given me a sense of grounding I didn't know I needed. It's made me see the value in finding peace with where I'm at, even if Dover is not my dream city.

As for my fashion dreams, I've started to dip my toes back in, experimenting with my and my son's outfits. It's a small step towards merging my love for fashion with skincare, something that feels uniquely me. Looking back, maybe stepping away from a career in fashion was for the best, but who says I can't blend my passions now?

LETTER TO SELF

Dear little Nikki,

Right now, you're feeling lost, hurt, and overwhelmed by what's currently going on in your life. You feel like no matter what you do, you just don't fit in. If you express yourself and be your authentic self, then it'll get worse. The teasing continues, even when you go along with it and start to call yourself those names. It doesn't matter. The verbal abuse that you experience from Mom doesn't make it better. You feel like you're not safe when you're home or with family, and sometimes you just want to run away. I want you to know it's not your fault. Don't blame yourself for other people's actions. I want you to know that the pain you're feeling is temporary, and it will get better.

You will learn as you get older that people take out their frustrations, feelings of inadequacy, and jealousy on those around them because they can't deal with themselves. You will learn that there's nothing wrong with not fitting in or not being liked. You're strong, unique, courageous, beautiful, and intelligent. Everything that you're going through has made you more resilient and stronger. Nikki, please give yourself permission to grow and not let this moment in your life define who you are and who you're going to be.

I know it seems rough right now, but I promise you that the journey you're on will be worth it. Acknowledge your feelings and keep moving. Your healing journey is just getting started. Understand that healing is a journey, not a destination. You will learn to love all your imperfections and understand that God created you for a purpose, on purpose. There will be people who will try to take you off your journey of becoming the woman you're meant to be. However, keep going and never give up. I promise it will get better, and the people who said you weren't going to be anything or called you ugly are going to eat those words.

Nikki, you will be great. Just continue to believe in yourself and always remember to love YOU. God doesn't make mistakes, and everything about you, He created. You are fearfully and wonderfully made.

With love and compassion

~ Nikki

CHAPTER EIGHT

More Than A Conqueror

Jasmine Oliver

I have been through quite some things in my young adult life. Looking back, I feel like God allowed me to go through these things to empathize with others, encourage them in the Lord, and pass down the wisdom and courage He has gifted me throughout the years. I have seen and tasted the goodness of the Lord. No matter my challenges, He was always with me and never failed. That is the nature of God. Because of Him, I can boldly say that I am more than a conqueror.

Here is a part of my story— a compilation of the most traumatic life lessons I endured between the ages of 18 and 20 years old. I call these my growing pain years. These were the most challenging yet pivotal years of my life and my walk with Jesus. These are some moments where my faith grew the most because I learned to push through the trials and tribulations of my youth. I felt like I never got a break in the midst of the storms.

God had to show me the areas of weakness I had that made me vulnerable and susceptible to pain and temptation. By wearing my heart on my sleeve, I became collateral damage to the deception and pain of others. I wanted to aid in their healing, and I was often willing to forgo my needs to accommodate them. But God never gave up on my healing. Because of His faithfulness and unfailing love, I am alive and well, growing in wisdom and discernment, placing better boundaries, and using greater judgment to make the right decisions in my life.

Through my journey with Jesus, I am learning what it truly means to love yourself and others— aiding in their healing but not compromising it for your own. That is a place I have always desired to be, but I have constantly struggled with trying to do it on my own. I still haven't arrived, but thankfully, today, I am one step closer. This is a part of my journey and a beautiful testimony of how God delivered me out of the tumultuous storm of my adolescence. I was born on a sunny Wednesday in Alexandria, Virginia, on June 21st, 2000–the first day of summer and the longest day of the year. (Fun fact ☺)

Shortly after my arrival into the world, my parents divorced, and my mother gained full custody of me. We moved to a three-story townhome in Maryland while my father settled into an apartment just fifteen minutes away. Those initial years of my life, spent in Baltimore County, are remembered as a foundation of love and learning. It was at the young age of 4 that Jesus found me. I heard the Gospel and believed He was who He said He was—the Son of God, my Lord, and my Savior. I evangelized at daycare, praised him in the house and the car, and familiarized myself with my picture Bible. I had many friends during these early years, yet a very stoic, quiet, and gentle nature.

Now, the real journey began when my mother and I moved to Delaware with the intent to be closer to her family. We relocated in the middle of my first-grade year, settling into a new single-family home—my favorite house ever. It was a project of love and choice as my mother, and I handpicked the renovations and furnishings, transforming it into a space that genuinely felt like our own. We lived in a semi-rural neighborhood—much different from Baltimore County. The house had a huge backyard, we turned one of the bedrooms into my playroom, and my mother had a state-of-the-art workout room. I had many sweet memories here—feeling safe, free, and comfortable in my environment.

As the years trickled by, we relocated when I was ten years old to a smaller but newly built townhouse in Bear, Delaware. Although slightly more compact, this house felt new and had its perks— a massive bedroom that felt like two rooms fused into one. The location truly won me over, placing me nearer to family, school, and delightfully, across the street from my favorite ice cream store.

However, the tone of my environment shifted during my sixth-grade year when I was around eleven years old. Economic pressures nudged us into a smaller townhome on the outskirts of Maryland. This house, unlike any before, struggled to feel like home. Its dim lights and persistent odor of cigarette smoke filled me with a deep sense of unease. There was something about that house that I did not like. The walls seemed to press in closer here, and the loss of space and a shared bathroom marked some inconvenient rule changes in my household. This place didn't just lack physical space; it lacked the warmth and security I had grown accustomed to.

By seventh grade, an opportunity arose with a job offer for my mom in New Jersey, and we moved to a new condo complex. The unit was on the third floor, offering a respite from the noise and a semblance of our desired peace. Though smaller, it had a modern touch, and I could walk to places where I could meet up with my friends. I felt a part of a community living in this town, and that sense of community was what I always longed for as a child.

I was technically an only child, navigating a world split between my divorced parents. But the reality of my family structure was layered with nuance. I stood alone on my mother's side but was the youngest child on my father's side. Before my parents met, my father had a daughter, my older half-sister, from his teenage years with another woman. Her mother later had another daughter with a different man. My father, a constant presence in his first daughter's life, embraced this other girl as his own, ensuring she never felt left out during his visits.

As a child, "half-sisters" never crossed my mind; they were my sisters. Although they lived in Philadelphia, we had mothers who saw eye to eye, and our fathers were committed to keeping us connected. Their mother even called me her "adopted daughter," treating me as one of her own. Philly, a city that held so much of my heart, felt like home. There, I felt the sense of community I craved, the freedom to hang out on the block, and the experiences that helped me to relate to my friends and classmates living in urban communities. Sometimes, I told them I was from Philly because I wanted to relate.

Ironically, I had the closest connection with my older sister's half-sister. For the longest time, I didn't even realize we weren't entirely blood-related. I adored her. She was my playmate and style icon, always there to play Bratz with me or put me on to the latest trends in pop culture. What I learned from her helped me feel less insular in my identity and gave me something to connect with my friends back at school.

However, as the years passed, seeing my sisters became increasingly difficult. My weekend visits with my father often ended with me begging him to drop me off in Philly. Sometimes, he would decline, citing fatigue or a desire to spend time just with me, which, at a young age, felt like a missed opportunity to be with my sisters. Over time, I adjusted my expectations, treasuring the shared moments with my father and being grateful for the times I saw my sisters.

Back home, I often pleaded with my mom for a sibling, dreaming of a little brother to fill the void I felt as an only child. She genuinely considered adoption, yet it never came to pass. But after 22 years, my prayers were unexpectedly answered. My father had another child, giving me a little brother. This new addition to my family, arriving so much later in my life, was a blessing that brought so much joy and redefined the meaning of family once more.

My relationship with my father started as the quintessential daddy-daughter bond—I adored him. He was the epitome of strength and coolness— born and raised in Philly and highly gifted and intelligent. He was the best dad anyone could ask for. He had a knack for technology and always kept me updated with the latest gadgets. He bought me my first iPod Mini, followed by an iPod Nano. Every week, I would compile a list of songs, and come the weekend, we'd spend hours together downloading music to my iPods. We shared memorable road trips to Atlanta, where he purchased a house but still chose to stay in Maryland to remain close to his daughters and mother. On one special trip, he even took me to the Cabbage Patch Museum, a magical experience for a little girl.

My father never went to college, but through sheer hard work and dedication, he earned as much as a college graduate, all with a high school diploma. I deeply admired him for his success, especially since he grew up without his father. He became a pillar of support for many around him—his daughters, mother, and girlfriends. The losses in his family, including the death of his middle brother and the absence of his eldest, increased my sympathy and understanding of the personal challenges he faced. He was a man striving to forge his identity while shouldering the responsibilities of many others.

I always knew my father loved me, but I questioned some of his decisions and behaviors. There were times that he would expose me to explicit music and images because he did not tailor much of his environment to a kid-friendly zone. As a child, I was highly intelligent and inquisitive, so I listened to every inappropriate lyric and analyzed every inappropriate album cover. Sometimes, I would ask him to turn off the song because it made me uncomfortable, and he usually would. He would then play my favorite gospel songs and have praise parties in the car.

However, he would usually continue to play certain explicit songs the next weekend or even the next day, and eventually, I got tired of asking him. I would sit, roll my eyes, or cover my ears until we were home. The drives usually weren't long. I was still living in Maryland, and he lived around the corner.

However, these were some of the formative and early years of my psyche development. I was very young, around five and six years old. Between the ages of four and fourteen, I met many women and children when I spent time with my father on the weekends. He had numerous girlfriends growing up, and many of them had children. I never really had an issue with the women he was seeing. Many of them took a liking to me and treated me as their children, sometimes even nicer. They would cook, do my hair, take me along shopping, and genuinely get to know me. There were some whose children I became so close with that they became another family unit--another adopted mom and more adopted siblings. I would be glad to see them on the weekends, and most of the time, I was okay with not spending time with my dad. He would often drop me off and "go handle business," picking up food for us and occasionally stopping by at random times throughout the weekend.

When I got older, my father and I bonded over philosophical hour-long phone calls and our love of food, jokes, and intellectual movies that we would watch with his girlfriend.

Another thing that marked our relationship was transparency and communication. He was willing to listen to my complaints, and he was willing to make changes when he could. My dad never tried to control me, but he genuinely listened to my perspective on issues, and there was mutual respect.

Now, my mother and I were inseparable, truly best friends. Our special thing, "Girl's Night Out," was the highlight of my week around the ages of four to six. Every Friday, she'd pick me up early, and we'd head to 7/11 for slushies and barbecue Fritos, sometimes hitting the park to chat or catch a movie, and other times, indulging in Baskin Robbins ice cream or hanging out at Pizza Hut. These outings were fun, carved out from her demanding job schedule, and remain some of my fondest memories with my mother as a little girl.

A profound openness and intimacy marked our relationship. I spent hours in her room from ages four to nine, asking countless questions. She encouraged honesty above all, assuring me that I would never be in trouble for telling the truth. These conversations nurtured our bond and equipped and protected me throughout my childhood. Every night before bed, she would sing "Jesus Loves Me" and gently rub my feet, a lullaby that filled those moments with laughter and pleaded for "just one more time."

The greatest gift my mother gave me, beyond the playroom that was my palace, was the introduction to faith. She brought me to church, shared Bible stories, and we prayed together nightly. She was vigilant about what I consumed, from books to television, ensuring everything I encountered was appropriate and enriching. Her commitment to my education was incredible. After picking me up from my afterschool program, she'd have creative writing assignments ready for me, fostering a love for reading and writing from a very young age. These weren't mere homework tasks but adventures in creativity that we explored together.

On our school drives, she filled our conversations with lessons on mortgages, insurance, and life skills, instilling in me the value of financial wisdom. Her journey, graduating debt-free from Harvard Law School, was a powerful testament to the virtues of hard work and smart financial planning, inspiring me to aspire to similar heights. My mother's influence extended beyond academic success; she instilled core values of integrity and respect. My youthful endeavors, from winning a coloring contest for a Mother's Day gift to publishing a book at age 10 with her support, were a testament to the confidence she fostered in me. Her presence was a constant during track meets and school events, pushing me to excel and celebrating every victory, no matter how small. Traveling to London and Paris, experiencing new cultures, and creating scrapbooks of our adventures, we lived life to the fullest, strengthening our bond with every shared experience. My mom was more than a parent; she was the epitome of love and dedication. She was my best friend.

As loving and endearing as our relationship was, it had its rougher patches as I neared adolescence. The values my mom had instilled in me were at war with the influences at work when I was away with my dad, away at school, and away at my afterschool programs. Before adolescence, I was more independent in thought, and the planted seeds didn't sprout or grow to substantially affect my life. However, during the years and stages of puberty, things became complicated. I became interested in the rules that were laid down, and I began to question them. My mom did not take this very lightly, and it caused intense strife and division among us. We stopped seeing eye to eye, and I felt a lot of pressure to do things to keep her happy, which began to diminish my self-worth. She started having struggles at work, and those things would come home with her, leading to outbursts, arguments, and unnecessary rage against me. I would say horrible things about her under my breath, and my heart became very cold towards her.

The relationship we had was unconventional at times. There were times she would cuss me out like a sister rather than discipline me as a daughter, and there were times that I could be so open with her about things that my friends would never be able to talk about with their moms. We didn't have a love-hate relationship, but we definitely had a love-judge relationship. When we weren't showing love to one another, we were often judgmental. That judgment of one another made it difficult for us to be vulnerable, and that led to us having many differences, opposing perspectives, and ultimately, miscommunications and misinterpretations that led to explosive, unnecessary, and utterly dramatic conflict.

As I sit back and reflect on the relationship between my mother and myself, I realize that our characteristic similarities may have influenced our conflicts. My mother is very passionate, determined, and unwavering when trying to prove a point. She is an attorney, after all. As I consider our interactions, I see that I have inherited these traits from her. We stood our ground when conflicts arose, often leading to intense disagreements. Despite the challenges, understanding this connection has given me a new perspective. Recognizing that we both share this passionate drive helps me appreciate her more deeply and allows me to see our conflicts differently.

As I continue to reflect, memories from my childhood begin to surface, bringing to light some of the trauma I experienced. I vividly recall a sunny day that turned physically, mentally, and emotionally dark once evening neared. I had no idea what was happening, but the next day, when I went to school, my grandmother picked me up from the Salvation Army instead of my mom. We drove straight to the hospital, and I had to stay in the car by myself. It was a long time filled with uncertainty, and I grew anxious about being left in the dark.

Eventually, my mother explained to me that my uncle had beaten his fiancée to death and that she died in the hospital from her injuries. He had turned himself into prison the same day it happened. My whole world was turned upside down. I was only ten years old. This was the first trauma that I had experienced in our family. I wasn't used to things of this nature happening so close to my reality. I felt torn, and it was a very dark time for me and my family because we had no idea what was going to happen, and the trauma of his ex-fiancée dying was brutal. They had children together, and she had children of her own. These kids were now orphaned; who would take them in? How would the court decide custody? Was my uncle going to receive the death penalty? Would I ever see my cousin who lived in Maryland again? She had a different mother, so how would her mother take this? Why would he do this? He seemed happy when I last saw him a couple of hours before he lashed out.

As a child, many questions and things did not make sense. I was devastated. I wanted everyone to be okay, and I wanted to see my cousin more than anything. She was my sister. When she visited, all we wanted to do was hang out with each other. Unfortunately, I didn't have a way to communicate with her for years. I could only pray for her and ask God to see her again. After four years of praying, she surprised me at my fourteenth birthday party at Dave and Buster's, and I cried when I got to see her again. It was a miracle. However, after losing contact with her again, we faced our traumas, and our relationship's innocence and wholesome nature were never the same, though our bond remains intact.

As a child, I coped with many stressful situations by trying to prepare myself and brace myself for things that I couldn't control. I had a lot of anxiety when I ran track and field outside of the comfort of my small Diocese of Wilmington League. I felt much pressure to win when running against regional and national competitors. I always strived to do my best, but because I was a part of an elite team, there was a burden to meet expectations that were no longer just my own. I

got placed into the 400m dash, a race I barely ran in school, but the race that would be coined as my best race throughout the summer of 2012. The pressure of rising in the rankings and competing on a national level took a toll on my mental health, and though I was winning and breaking personal records, I never had any peace. Practices were incredibly challenging, and my coach was an Olympic-style coach. My summer felt like a track boot camp, and I always had a lump in my throat when I thought about all the pressure I had to perform. I did not crack or fold under pressure, but I tried sometimes. My mom would push me to keep going because she knew I could make it to the finish line, no pun intended.

Eventually, when I told my coach I wanted to drop out before our regional meet, she gave me a speech letting me know that I was not quitting on her watch. I had to brace for the storm because I couldn't avoid it. I just had to do it to get to the other side. At times, I would run three or four times a day just to come back and compete the next day; I couldn't complain because there was nothing to do and nowhere to go but through. This took a toll on my mental health, but it cultivated a key mindset of never quitting and always seeing things through, even the things that are the most challenging. I am so grateful that I never stopped and left with something to show for all the hard work and dedication I put into that summer.

I saw quitting as a form of failure and forced myself to become comfortable with being uncomfortable. These moments tested my faith as a child and strengthened my relationship with God. I would always pray to myself, quote scriptures, and remain focused on the finish line. That has become one of my greatest metaphors for life. My concern was not to win but to do my best and get it over with. My grounding Scriptures as a child and teenager were Philippians 4:13 and "This too shall pass." And no matter what I went through, the storm would always pass, and eventually, there would always be a rainbow. This mindset got me through some of the hardest things in my life that were to come.

As a young girl, I was timid. In front of others, particularly adults, I was quiet, calm, and reserved. In my alone time, I was often content, keeping myself busy reading books, drawing, playing computer games, listening to music, and playing with my Bratz dolls. Around my friends, I was more outgoing, loving to play and make up fun games, dance to music, and laugh at the silly things they would do.

My childhood was very nuanced. I lived in suburban communities, yet all my friends were from urban communities because of my school, after-school programs, and the women my father dated. I also had a strong spiritual foundation because of my mother and the urban Catholic school she placed me in from first to seventh grade. I learned to adapt as a young girl and relate to many different types of people from various backgrounds.

I was often viewed as the smart kid, the good kid, and the talented kid. I was one of the most well-behaved and mannerly—making me a favored student of many teachers, and I got a lot of attention for my artwork, intelligence, and kindness from my peers.

As I transitioned into middle school, I became self-conscious about my appearance and identity. As puberty hit, there was a shift towards physical characteristics and popularity. I was well-known but not the most outgoing and charismatic—I was quiet and sweet. I was pretty, and guys crushed on me, but I didn't get attention for how I looked as much as for who I was. As silly as that sounds to complain about, I craved the attention of being cool, funny, and beautiful. I wanted to be fashionable, bold, and free, and I wanted to be grown like the kids around me.

I was becoming more influenced by the characteristics of my friends, and I wanted to fit in more, but I was feeling the increasing burden of being set apart. I was a high achiever and was ultimately from the suburbs, no matter how much I tried to spin the narrative with my weekend escapades with my father. My mother was stricter than most of the parents of my peers, and I was not allowed to wear or be exposed to certain things on her watch. This caused me to be sneaky and watch certain movies and television shows when she was not around. I continued to keep up an impression among my teachers and after-school counselors. Still, I was juggling the growing desire to be grown like everybody else—the pressure of being the center of attention for "being good" started to get to me. I was seen as an example in the eyes of adults, but I wanted to be seen as an equal to my peers.

I often compared their freedom with the freedom I wanted to live outside of the box of my mother's approval. Life became a double-edged sword. I got way more grace than the other kids around me because my teachers knew my character and integrity, deeming that when I did something "wrong," there was likely a valid reason. But to my mom, my mistakes seemed far more disappointing because of the expectation that I knew better and my consistency in doing better. The feeling of disappointing my mother and failing to meet expectations consistently kept me very disciplined, low-risk, and out of trouble. But the times I struggled to remain disciplined, I kept my secrets hidden in the dark and guarded my "angelic" image by lying and being sneaky about certain vices behind closed doors.

Around this time, I often compared myself to other people. I appreciated the looks and personality of others more, idolizing how God made them and praying and asking Him to please change me. I was faithfully awaiting my glow-up season— the season when puberty would hit, and I would look as pretty as the older girls I looked up to in real life and on TV.

In terms of social challenges and stressors, my greatest coping mechanism was to adapt. I would have to adjust to new environments, and eventually, my environment began to change so much that I would shift to conform. After transferring to many schools in such a short period, I would become a floater. I would have many friends and hang out with multiple friend groups. I could hang onto my individuality for a while, but as I continued through adolescence, the pressure to conform began to clash with the pressure to stand out. I didn't know who I was or who I wanted to be. I stood out because I had no choice. My mom was overprotective of me, so I had to embrace being unique even when I felt like an outsider. I couldn't express myself how I wanted to, but I had to do what was pleasing or required. I coped with this by adopting an ideal identity of myself in my head, vowing to become the person I always wanted to be when I was 18.

It wasn't until we moved to Jersey that I became more nuanced in my identity. The complexity of my childhood was settling in as I learned to adapt to a new environment in the middle of the school year, three different times in seventh grade. As I got more accustomed to the culture in Jersey, I got to reforge my unique identity—leaving the past one behind. My first experience was in a public school, where the culture was much more relaxed than in a private school. I permitted myself to share the jokes and do the goofy things I used to keep to myself in my head. I began breaking out of my shell quickly and becoming the social butterfly I constantly desired to be.

Moving to Jersey gave me the freedom to break free from the precedent of my past and to be the person I always felt that I was deep down inside—an actual cool kid who happened to be smart, kind, and gifted. Around this time, my style was evolving into a more unique expression of my identity. I thrifted clothes from Plato's Closet, a saving grail to my confidence because my mom refused to buy the other kids' brand-name clothes.

My mom earned a considerable living wage but was very frugal and wise with her money. She was quicker to spend on an enriching experience or opportunity and slow to spend on material things like Jordan's and Nike tee-shirts. I didn't understand or appreciate it as a child, but it forced creativity and uniqueness to emerge, and I learned to be content with what I had. I learned to embrace my influence on my creative expression in clothing, hairstyles, and music. Rather than just impressing others with my athletic and academic performance, I impressed people with my unique sense of style, my underground taste in music, and my latest knowledge of pop culture.

I was becoming a leader who influenced others with charisma rather than a black sheep who stood out for being different but often felt invisible simultaneously—as if my presence didn't truly matter to my peers. God was answering my prayers, and the glow-up I was waiting for was taking root as I started to become the girl I always wanted to be as a child.

As I became more comfortable in my skin, I became more outgoing. I started to crave that attention and interaction with others more. Being further away from my family, not seeing my sisters often, and being in a new location increased that void of community. My mother's stricter boundaries prevented me from being as social as I wanted. I felt she didn't understand me because she didn't have that same desire for spontaneity and community.

My sudden evolution presented a newfound challenge for her as well. I wanted more freedom and was more willing to fight for it. This started to cause a very big rift between us as my repentance from timidity was viewed by her as a lack of gratitude and respect, while I viewed her unexplained reasonings as irrational and controlling. Routinely feeling trapped by rules and judgment perpetuated a strong desire to want to get away. I loved my mom deeply, but I wanted the freedom to grow in my new identity without being compared to the precedent of my past as a little girl.

Boarding school was a perfect compromise that I came up with because of the community structure and freedom I craved, as well as the prestigious education that my mother preferred for me. Surprisingly, boarding school was one of the best decisions that ever happened to me. My mom and I got so much closer, becoming best friends again and respecting each other's boundaries, though we lived in different places. I only lived twenty minutes away from home, so I could still see her, and we would frequently go to church and get our nails done, bonding and catching up on my adventures throughout the week.

Boarding school also gave me a sense of structure and community I didn't have before and a very innovative and educational experience where I could grow. The closeness that I felt by being around my friends so casually increased my happiness, helped me find my place, and provided me with the intimacy of new sisters and brothers that I could laugh with, confide in, and learn from. Since I lived with the people I saw daily, there was no way to have it together all the time. Mistakes were inevitable, and I experienced the beauty of grace in my living and learning environment. However, the pressure taken off to perform for my mom's approval now became for the approval of others. I worked hard to prove that I belonged at the institution and that, as a black female student, I was no lesser than the rich students of other ethnicities.

It was very important to me to prove my prestige, keeping almost a 4.0 GPA, visiting and applying to schools such as Duke, Harvard, and Yale, and having huge dreams to build a major legacy such as being the first black woman commissioner of the

NBA. I also worked hard to prove to the black community that I was attractive. A lot of the boys at my school were into dating girls of other ethnicities instead—speaking down on black women. I felt the need to put my best foot forward every day.

I genuinely loved my appearance and the freedom to experiment with makeup, hairstyles, and fashion. However, my identity started to gravitate to how I looked and dressed. Once I set a precedent for being one of the attractive girls, I felt like I couldn't have an off day. I wanted to look perfect for class and in the evenings when class was over. I wanted everything I did to look effortless, yet I put so much effort into looking flawless.

I was discovering a new part of myself that I never knew existed as a child. I was experiencing the freedom I always desired but became consumed with the next greatest thing. Boarding school started to feel too restrained because of the rules that no longer fit my ambitious agenda. I started comparing my level of independence with some of the other students whose parents gave the school permission for them to go on overnight weekend trips. I wanted to hang out with my friends on overnight trips and leave campus for more than school-sponsored outings.

Around this time, I unknowingly had a problem with submitting to authority. When rules felt like irrational boundaries and rigid policies, I automatically felt controlled. Anything that made me feel controlled almost instantly frustrated me and caused me to want to rebel. Rules that didn't align with what I deemed as sensible deeply agitated me, and I would challenge the things that didn't make sense to me. I was rebellious with just intentions, and I fought for what I believed in and advocated for the things that mattered most to me.

When I went to church, I would hear the Word, feel convicted, and then decide deep down inside that I probably should change. However, I loved the new identity I had cultivated since moving to Jersey. I never wanted to move back to Delaware, and I never wanted to go back to feeling "lame" and alone. Being set apart and feeling insular at a young age was hard. I was finally fitting in with others by following my path and creating influence by being my authentic self. I was showing all of me: the sweet, the spicy, and the savory.

After feeling controlled for so long, all I wanted to do was be in the driver's seat of my own life. I was intelligent, and with many decisions I made, I could avoid harsh consequences. Things worked out in my favor by doing my own thing, so I had confidence in my ability to navigate my own world. Ironically, my pride and complacency led me straight into the storm of my youth and ultimately to the growing pains of reality. I call this chapter of my life: Welcome to the Real World Girlfriend.

I was adventurous and open-minded in my early years, eagerly embracing new experiences without rigid opinions. This openness allowed me to absorb diverse perspectives with ease. However, during college, as I confronted the narrative of an "unstable upbringing," my perception of myself began to shift dramatically. What I once viewed as resilience—my ability to swiftly move on from challenges—started to feel like unaddressed trauma. My spontaneity and impulsiveness, once sources of joy, seemed to reflect a lack of discipline and self-control. This deep dive into my past forced me to scrutinize every fragment of my personality, and I found myself beginning to resent aspects of myself that I had once cherished. I blamed myself for my perceived shortcomings and for every negative experience I endured, viewing my identity as inherently flawed, constructed from a foundation of brokenness and identity confusion.

As I reflect on my life, I see that I've had a lot of sexual trauma. I lost my virginity when I was 15 years old to a 19-year-old boy, and I was sexually assaulted by a close friend and a guy I met at a party. I was sexually harassed by my driving instructor and by my managers at Walmart. A guy tried to rape me in the shower while I was on vacation in Costa Rica with my best friend, and I trusted a guy that gave me herpes.

This all started during my freshman year in college. After matching with a guy on Tinder, I connected with him. He took his time getting to know me, sending cute messages that stood out from the rest. After about two weeks of texting, we finally hung out in person. He was funny, easygoing, and seemed genuinely interested in getting to know me rather than just wanting to sleep with me. In the beginning, he didn't try to rush anything. Eventually, I stayed the night with him, and we became intimate. The first time, he asked if he could remove the condom midway through our encounter, and I told him no. I felt he might try to remove it anyway, so I told him to stop. As we spent more time together and frequently engaged in intimacy, I began to trust him and eventually allowed him to have sex with me without protection.

One night, he hosted a game night for my friends and me. He provided the food, and we had a great time full of laughter. My friends thought he was cool when they first met him. I became more comfortable with him and would go to his place to hang out and do my homework. He ensured I was well taken care of and was low maintenance, just wanting to spend time together. I noticed it was always dark at his place. He kept his blackout curtains up even during the day, so I never knew what time it was, and the days seemed to fly by. Since I had no Monday or Friday classes, I decided to stay with him the whole weekend. My friends were busy with their plans, making it more practical to stay with him.

During this particular stay, his roommate jokingly told me that "Trouble" (his nickname) had AIDS, had about six children, and was 30 years old. Alarmed, I immediately asked him if any of this was true and requested to see his driver's license. He made excuses and accused me of trusting his friend more than him, who he said tended to joke about many things. After discovering some troubling information about my boyfriend, I confronted him. My mother found a DUI record showing his birthdate, revealing that he was 27 years old, not 30, as his roommate had jokingly claimed. Despite my friends' advice to stop seeing him, I returned to him again. The next day, I returned to my room on campus, but soon after, I was in extreme pain and could barely move. I called my mother, describing my symptoms, and she immediately flew out to be with me.

I went to the campus doctor, who examined me and suspected it was the herpes simplex virus. She suggested getting tested for HIV, but I declined. When my mother arrived, we went to a hospital to address the other issues causing my pain, including a UTI that turned into a yeast infection after antibiotics and a tear that made it excruciatingly painful to use the bathroom. About a week after my mother left, the test results confirmed that I had herpes, and I was devastated. I called my mother, who reassured me everything would be okay. I confronted my boyfriend, but he denied knowing anything about it and insisted I must have contracted it from someone else. He didn't treat me any differently but refused to get tested himself. Initially, I isolated myself from him due to his lies and deception. Still, eventually, I reconnected with him through phone calls and texts, feeling like he was the only person who understood what I was going through.

During this traumatic period, I was overwhelmed with fear and anxiety. I searched through his cabinets for medications and paid close attention to his phone calls, questioning more about his past. Despite everything, my feelings for him remained strong. He was the first man who made me feel wanted all the time, answered every call, cared for me physically, protected me, and never switched up on me in public. He didn't drink or smoke, and he always ensured I was safe after nights out. He was loyal, easy to talk to, and the most handsome man I had ever been with. I deeply cared for him and wanted to believe in his goodness.

The diagnosis left me distraught, embarrassed, deeply wounded, and insecure. I thought I would be tied to him forever, and no one else would ever want to be with me. I experienced intense regret and the crushing realization that I couldn't fix or return from this. I felt like my life was over, stained forever, and I spiraled into depression, even contemplating suicide. The shock and betrayal were overwhelming, and I felt fearful and anxious about my future.

At the time, I was too afraid to get tested for HIV, living with constant anxiety about whether I would even live to see 25. I felt embarrassed, stupid, isolated, and regretful for allowing this to happen. My emotions ranged from extreme anger and sadness to confusion, as I had never encountered someone who could lie and manipulate so easily without remorse. He had no empathy for his impact on my life, and I felt hopeless and endangered by a man I once thought was the best I had ever had.

The entire experience left me vulnerable, depressed, and weak, struggling to cope with the intense and painful emotions. I was stuck in bed for days because it hurt so much to move, and I was overwhelmed with extreme pain and embarrassment. My mom flew to Florida to be with me. She encouraged me by sharing her traumas, letting me know I was not alone. She stayed with me while I was in the hospital, and when I felt better, she took me out and bought me food. Her presence cheered me up and reassured me that I needed to make it through each day.

After my mom left, a friend on campus took care of me, buying me food and checking in on me regularly. Despite this support, I felt isolated from my initial friend group and couldn't turn to them for support. I lost motivation and wasn't comfortable sharing what I was going through, so I had to fight through the pain to appear okay. During this time, I had floated into another friend group, tied together through partying and lighthearted adventures. However, still fighting depression, I withdrew whenever possible and slept a lot until the new friends I had made forced me to get up. I had nightmares and was anxious about the possibility of having AIDS. I felt suicidal, fearing I had a life-threatening disease.

I told my mom it felt pointless to live if I had to carry this burden forever. She encouraged me in the Lord, advising me to take it one day at a time and be proud of each small victory. She prayed for me and expressed her confidence that I did not have HIV, which helped me find hope in God's grace and His mercy. I felt remorse for my sins and questioned if God would spare me from the consequences of my actions, as I had defied His will by having sex outside of marriage. My family always told me, "You are different. You can't do what everybody else can do." This became a harsh reality when my participation in what seemed like normal college activities led to extreme, life-altering consequences. Yet, I always thanked God because it could have been much worse.

After speaking to my mom, I dreamed of an angel, a white light floating above me, and I heard the Lord tell me I would be okay. This gave me the courage to get tested for HIV, and when the results came back negative, I was immensely relieved. I finally felt hope and confidence to move forward. I experienced God's faithfulness firsthand in the midst of my trauma.

Throughout this time, God sent many angels to love me. At this time, my core friend group stopped hanging out with me because they found my situation too much to handle emotionally. However, one friend remained by my side, offering unconditional love and acceptance without judgment. She supported me through everything, even though I didn't open up about all that had happened. She was an angel God placed in my life to remind me that I was not a mess but a person who needed love.

Shortly after discovering everything, there was a hurricane warning that fall semester. My roommate and her friends invited me to stay with them at a friend's house in Jacksonville, so I wouldn't have to go back home. Although I didn't want to participate in the partying, being around kind people and staying active kept me from sinking into depression and suicidal thoughts. My dad connected me with my oldest sister's godmother during that time. She took me to the park and out for food. We explored the city and tried Thai food for the first time. We laughed and took many pictures, experiencing lighthearted happiness without drugs, liquor, or parties.

Throughout that week, I reached out to the man I had been with, as I felt a deep soul tie to him. He was the only one I could confide in during late nights when I felt discouraged. I found out he had two children, and he finally admitted to these truths. The lies were exposed, and I stopped sleeping with him. However, learning more about his story as a foster child, I found compassion to forgive him and move on.

Shortly after this experience, I was taken advantage of by two different men. As I was regaining hope and rebuilding my confidence to make new friends and finish my first semester of college on a positive note, I became open and trusting again. I was invited to smoke with a guy I met over the summer, someone I considered a friend. Although I knew he had been interested in me before, I thought he understood that nothing could happen between us, especially since I had dated his roommate. There was some tension between us because he had expressed interest first, but I was uninterested and chose to date his roommate instead. I thought his invitation was an extension of an olive branch, and up to that point, I had never experienced a guy smoking with me for any reason other than to get high.

I told my new friends, who were all excited for me, making jokes about how they would love to smoke with him. I assured them there was nothing between us and that I would see them later when I returned. I had no intention of staying the night. When he picked me up, everything seemed normal. However, when I arrived at his house, I noticed that everyone was gone, just the two of us. He told me he didn't know how to roll a blunt, so we joked and laughed, Facetiming our friends and watching videos on how to do it. At one point, the weed spilled, and I now think that was an escape God provided, but I was just happy to reconcile with my friend and get high for free. We picked up the weed, rolled the blunt, and watched a movie.

As it got dark, I asked if he could take me home. He said he was tired and asked if I would mind staying. I didn't want to, but my friends didn't have a car, and I figured I could save money on an Uber. I trusted him. High out of my mind, I just needed a place to sleep. I asked if he could sleep on the couch while I took his bed, but he insisted we could both sleep in the bed without anything happening. I asked if his roommate was coming home, and he said he didn't think so. Rather than trust my gut and go home, I trusted his words and believed we could share the bed without any issues.

When I walked into the dark room, I banged my foot on the side of his bed—another warning sign. As I tried to sleep, he wouldn't let me. He kept bothering me and eventually was naked, asking me to perform oral sex. He tried to push my head down, and I constantly refused, asking what was wrong with him. He got angry, mentioning how I had chosen his roommate over him and questioning why I would do it for his roommate but not for him. I felt disgusted and trapped. I told him I didn't like him and that he needed to get over it. Instead, he decided to have sex with me. I screamed at him to put on a condom and just braced myself, crying and asking God why these things kept happening to me. I had just physically healed and was on the verge of mental healing, but it felt like all my progress was being undone. I saw myself in his mirror, just hanging off the bed as he used my body to satisfy his ego, and I felt my soul leave my body as I realized I was being raped for the first time.

I always thought sexual assault involved a stranger, someone unattractive, or a situation with a gun to my head. None of this was true. It was someone close to me, someone many women lusted over, and it happened through mental manipulation. I blamed myself for so long for not kicking, screaming, or forcing him off me. I felt guilty for going in the first place. Afterward, I tried to convince myself that I should be happy to have slept with one of the finest guys on campus. But my soul hated every second of it. I hated watching myself lay lifeless, keeping it a secret, and pretending everything was fine in front of others. I hated that I blamed myself and let him go scot-free, even though my "No" should have been enough.

This experience taught me about the responsibility of accountability. Just because I walked into a compromised situation, blinded by my naivete and trust, didn't mean I deserved to be taken advantage of. I knew others had experienced what I considered worse, where they had no choice at all, which made me feel guilty for considering myself a victim. I decided to avoid him as much as possible without telling anyone, attempting to let God heal me again.

A couple of weeks later, a similar encounter happened with another man I met at a party from a nearby school. Despite everything, he convinced me to let him take me on a tour of his school. He had a car, so I didn't have to pay for an Uber, which scared me at the time. When it got dark, he took me to the dorms instead of touring the campus. I questioned why, and he said it was because it was dark. I asked why he picked me up then, considering the tour was all I came for. It was another trap, and I was so broken that I walked right into it.

This encounter was the most embarrassing and humiliating I had ever experienced. I had confided in him about what had happened to me, thinking it would help him as he talked about his fear of contracting something. Instead, he condemned me, telling me how pretty I was and how it was a shame. He said he didn't want to sleep with me, but then he chose to anyway, even though I didn't want to. It was horrible. He washed himself with a Clorox wipe afterward, and I asked him to take me home. He was too tired. I decided to call an Uber first thing in the morning when it was light outside.

I woke up in the middle of the night with this man attempting to have sex between my breasts. I was so disgusted and humiliated. I told him to get off of me and called an Uber immediately. I was left feeling ashamed, broken, confused, and disappointed that I had no backbone when it came to letting men use me. I was sick and tired of letting them treat me like an object, and my confidence felt shattered. It was nobody but God that kept me alive because I felt empty inside. When I got back to my room, I cried and cried, trying to be as quiet as possible so my roommate wouldn't hear me. I didn't feel like a victim but like a fool. I was sick and tired of feeling used, abused, and broken because of my lack of boundaries and discernment.

During my sophomore year in college, I started to feel defeated, careless, and numb, trying to forge my path and being let down multiple times. I turned to New Age healing practices to form a heightened spiritual and personal relationship with God. As a result of the deception of the occultic practices, I was enduring more spiritual abuse than I ever had in any religious setting in church. I felt healed from the anger and the rage, and my heart had truly softened again toward believing God's love and kindness for me. I was being taught about energy, vibrations, and the power of our thoughts over our reality. My voice became softer, and my speech was less aggressive; I began to accept myself more and focused on the positive side rather than constantly feeling like someone in the world was always against me. I experimented in a relationship with a masculine woman, who happened to be an occultic witch. I was so intrigued by the spiritual realities of life that I was oblivious to many of the dark things happening around me and even in her presence.

I just desired to escape the pain of everyday life that I chose to ignore responsibilities and obligations to fuel a false sense of peace and comfort induced by marijuana, acid, and counterfeit love. Not to mention, this experience occurred toward the time of COVID-19 lockdowns, so I had nothing to do but go on a spiritual escapade of healing and unraveling. However, the healing and unraveling that I was doing was not rooted in true worship and intimacy with God. I was building my new life on sand rather than the Rock, and when the storm came, which it did, it came faster than I ever could have imagined and harder than any other storm I had encountered before. But in this moment of chaos, God did the impossible, and I thank Him for saving me and sheltering me from the storm. After this moment, I realized that life could be dangerous, which was a touchy subject. I had endured some dark times previously, but nothing along the lines of the danger I endured coming into and out of that relationship with drugs, witchcraft, and idolatry. I had no idea any of those things were mentioned as sins in the Bible, and I certainly never regarded my behaviors as paganism. This experience truly shifted my reality of the world through a more Biblical lens rather than a lens solely based on my personal experiences with Jesus.

God rescued me from that nightmare experience by sending my mom, my stepfather, and my grandmother to Tallahassee to get me; I was placed in the hospital and a rehabilitation facility to detox off of the drugs that my ex-partner had unknowingly given to me. Being released from the rehabilitation center after just 11 days, I had a job interview the following week at a store in the mall that my mother had applied to on my behalf. I received the job with flying colors, and I was so grateful to God that He was helping me to get back on my feet.

I learned I had to sit with Him and slow down for God to heal my wounds. I couldn't run to the things I used to, seemingly good or bad, to heal me. I made so many messes in trusting in a man, or new clothes, or a business opportunity, or drugs, and alcohol to save me. I even turned to my beauty to feel better about myself because many times, by the grace of God, I did not look like what I had been through or was going through. The mask of beauty hid so much pain that it deeply lay within me. I convinced myself that if I looked good, I was good. I was so good at covering up my pain and convincing myself that I wasn't broken that I went through periods where I was unable even to cry. I would cry loudly and shed two or three streams of tears, and then I would straighten up my face and tell myself that everything was okay. I was very numb to pain and rigid to my emotions—desiring to escape my reality and run from the things that caused me discomfort—addressing and confronting my pain.

Through God's willingness to help and teach me along the way, I learned that there is no sweeter escape than Jesus. I take solace in His love being enough to fill the shattered cracks of my brokenness, and I know that I am whole because of the blood that Jesus Christ shed for me. I am not a fool. I am an overcomer through Christ, and the Gospel has a deeper meaning in my life because of my mistakes. I learned that boundaries protect and that God's will is to keep me safe. I am free to love openly but with boundaries, and I have joy and hope from Him alone.

Thank you for reading my testimony of what Jesus has done for me and the hope and restoration that abounds in His wisdom, grace, and eternal protection through salvation.

Psalm 23 KJV "The Lord is my shepherd; I shall not want. He maketh me to lie down in green pastures: he leadeth me beside the still waters. He restoreth my soul: he leadeth me in the paths of righteousness for his name's sake. Yea, though I walk through the valley of the shadow of death, I will fear no evil: for thou art with me; thy rod and thy staff they comfort me. Thou preparest a table before me in the presence of mine enemies: thou anointest my head with oil; my cup runneth over. Surely goodness and mercy shall follow me all the days of my life: and I will dwell in the house of the Lord forever"

LETTER TO SELF

Beloved Lil' Jasmine,

Remember your favorite quote?

> "Our deepest fear is not that we are inadequate. Our
> deepest fear is that we are powerful beyond measure. It
> is our light not our darkness that most frightens us. We
> ask ourselves, Who am I to be brilliant, gorgeous,
> talented, fabulous? Actually, who are you not to be? You
> are a child of God. Your playing small does not serve the
> world. There is nothing enlightened about shrinking so
> that other people won't feel insecure around you. We
> are all meant to shine, as children do. We were born to
> make manifest the glory of God that is within us. It's not
> just in some of us; it's in everyone. And as we let our
> own light shine, we unconsciously give other people
> permission to do the same. As we are liberated from our
> own fear, our presence automatically liberates others."
>
> ~ Marianne Williamson

I promise you'll come back to this quote years later and
fall in love with it all over again. Jasmine, you are brilliant,
you are kind, you are gorgeous. You are gifted beyond
measure with talents that you haven't discovered yet, but in
due season, you will. You are God's beautiful creation, and
you are meant to reflect the radiance of His glory. You

haven't discovered your purpose in life; you struggle at times with your identity, and that's okay. It will come to you in God's perfect timing.

I know you feel the pressure to keep it all together and to never disappoint those who you love most, but you were never designed to carry the burden of perfection. You are entitled to your own mistakes, and God has forgiven you through them all— using each one as a stepping stone for His greater purpose.

Don't be afraid to love yourself. You can be so focused on the good you see in others that you forgot to see the love on the inside of you. In fact, it is the love of God within you that will overcome the darkness that tries to overtake you.

You don't need to overcompensate for your past to be forgiven. God has already forgiven you, and your past does not define who you are. You are worthy of the same love. Forgive those who hurt you, including yourself. You have permission to overcome—relinquish the old, and take in the new. The Lord will do a new thing, and He will make you unrecognizable to your past mistakes. Part of embracing the new, is accepting what is without constantly trying to change yourself, and everything around you. You are enough. The world needs you to be exactly who you are.

Be free caged bird. The love that you were seeking for so long, has found you.

~ Jasmine

LETTER TO READERS

Beloved reader,

You are so much stronger than you know. You may not have known all that you were gonna face, but by the grace of God, you are more than a conqueror. God saw the end from the beginning and He still chose you. He predestined you and He foreknew you. He anointed you for the trials that you would face because He knew that you would lean to Him to overcome, and He would never leave you, nor forsake you in the process.

I may have heard your story, or maybe, I have not. But one thing I know about you is that you are not alone, and no matter what your situation has been you are not the only one. I struggled with feeling like I was the only one for a very long time. This caused me to experience anxiety, depression, insecurity, and low-self esteem. But through the strength of vulnerability and the divine reshaping of my identity through Christ, the Lord set me free.